Mist of Tears

Mist of Tears

The Life and Times of Mary McRae and Charles Magee

Roger Clark

For Pat McRae and her remarkable family

Introduction

On Dominion Day 1911, a single bullet fired by Farquhar McRae took the life of a young Scotsman. The event shocked the whole Glengarry community in Eastern Ontario and ultimately reverberated throughout Canada. More than one hundred years have gone by and yet many of the circumstances surrounding the murder have remained hidden or left in obscure corners of McRae family history. For the past ten years, I have attempted to piece together the full story, or at least as much as it has been possible for me to unearth. It has proved to be a fascinating journey into the lives, fortunes, and misfortunes of those who were involved, directly or indirectly, in this profound and complicated family tragedy.

Inevitably, there remain gaps and unanswered questions. It is my hope that, by making the results of my research available to others, the story may continue towards completion. History, with its multiple dimensions, deepens and expands with each step towards understanding, often raising more questions than it answers. On the other hand, an exploration of the actors, their characters, motivations, psychology, and the general circumstances of their lives allows us to get a little closer to knowing the reality of a crucial part of their story. At times, it seems to resemble a continually changing jigsaw puzzle, the pieces of which take on a life of their own, reshaping the picture and opening up new possibilities and fresh dimensions. Maybe the puzzle will never be completed, but it has been a rewarding challenge to put together some of the life and times of Mary McRae and Charles Magee.

Genealogy sometimes comforts us with the knowledge that family names have an infamous variety of spelling, signaling nothing more than popular confusion or ignorance within a largely oral tradition. In Glengarry County, it was (and still is) a widely held belief that the way a name is spelled may reflect religious affiliation. Thus, "Mac" is sometimes assumed to belong to a Protestant family (typically found in North Glengarry), whereas "Mc" is the flag-bearer for a proud Catholic dynasty (more often found in South Glengarry). It is also said that "Mc" belongs to the Highland tradition whereas "Mac" denotes Lowland origins. While these may reflect little more than popular beliefs, in the story of Mary McRae they reveal important social and emotional undercurrents. After her marriage to Charles, she became Mary Magee. By 1916, however, she was regularly using "Mary McGee", the form that she kept for the rest of her life. Her 'In Memoriam prayer card' reads "In loving memory of Mary McGee". Her son's gravestone bears the inscription "Charles Joseph McGee", although he was baptised in the Glen Nevis Church on 7 May 1911 as "Charles Stewart Alexander Magee". It was never clear where the name "Joseph" came from, but it has a strong Catholic resonance. "McGee" is more of a Scottish rather than an Irish name.

Key sources of information for this narrative have come from contemporary local newspapers which are listed in the Bibliography. Newspaper accounts of the most significant events, particularly those involving dramatic court cases, were often lengthy and detailed, providing readers with both sensational and mundane aspects of the story. The same problems afflicting news reporting that we know today applied equally in the early years of the last century. Fake news, biased interpretations, and straightforward fabrication were not unknown, particularly in the case of weekly newspapers which found themselves trying to 'catch up' with events that were already long over and done with.

News stories printed in one of the bigger papers were often reprinted more or less verbatim by other publications across Canada. Wire services did not yet exist, and *The Canadian Press* was only established in 1917. My task was to sort through the many versions of events as reported by different news sources and come up with a reasonably accurate summary of what took place. In some instances, I identify a specific newspaper, but, more often, I have chosen to incorporate quotations without encumbering the story with details of a specific source. I will happily provide relevant information if any reader requests it.

Finally, a word about the title, *Mist of Tears*. In December 1933, Mary sent a 1928 edition of Francis Thompson's magnificent 1893 poem, *The Hound of Heaven*, to her niece, Anna Margaret. She inscribed the gift as follows: *You already have a fine appreciation of this literary gem. May the years increase your appreciation of Thompson's masterpiece. Love from your Aunt Mary McGee. Dec 25, 1933.* She inserted a prayer card: *May Saint Joseph keep you all your life in the love of Jesus.*

Her choice of gift and her admiration for Thompson's poem tell us something of Mary's own character. The importance of Catholicism to her is evident and it must have remained a major source of the inner strength that she showed throughout her life. It may also be that she carried within her a sense of guilt, having turned away from her spiritual home during the years spent with Charles. Yet her faith pursued her and brought her back to salvation.

The title of this book is taken from the opening lines of *The Hound of Heaven*:

> *I fled Him, down the nights and down the days;*
> *I fled Him, down the arches of the years;*
> *I fled Him, down the labyrinthine ways*
> *Of my own mind; and in the mist of tears*
> *I hid from Him ...*

Clan McRae

The Rev. Farquhar MacRae, born in 1580, was Constable of Eilean Donan Castle. The lineage of the McRae family stretches much farther back into the 'dark ages' of the late-14th century, when they settled in the district of Kintail in the southwest of the county of Ross in the Scottish Highlands. History tells us that the McRaes came originally from Ireland several hundred years earlier.

Eilean Donan Castle, as it stands today, visited and photographed by millions of tourists, is largely a 20th-century reconstruction completed in 1932

following its purchase in 1911 by John MacRae-Gilstrap. The Castle remains in the care of the MacRae family and visitors are invited to sign one of two guestbooks: one for anyone of MacRae heritage, the other for everyone else. The original Castle, which dates from the early-13th century, grew in size and importance until it was destroyed following the Jacobite uprisings of the 17th and 18th centuries.

It is easy to understand the pride and fierce traditions of the Clan McRae, which are alive and well today. Having lived through the harsh 'clearances', the McRaes were part of the first major wave of immigrants coming to Canada in the very early years of the 19th century. They joined many other 'Highlanders' who came over with Bishop Alexander Macdonell and settled in Glengarry, more specifically in what is now Glen Nevis and Bridge End (Lancaster Township).

On 23rd June 1804, John McRae was granted the deed to "Lot Number Thirteen in the Sixth Concession of the said Township of Lancaster".

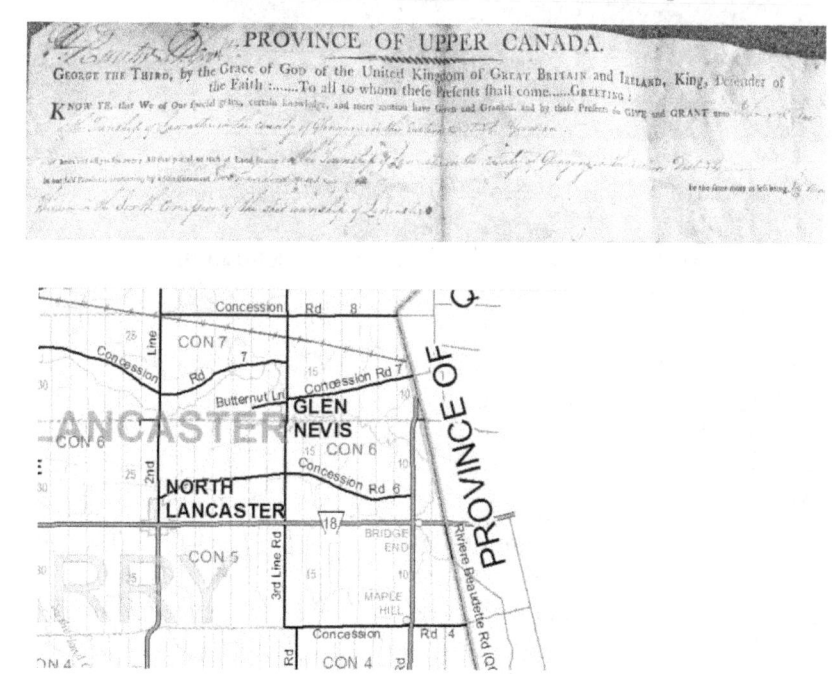

This became the home of the McRaes and remains in the family today. It is widely known as the 'Brick House'. About one hundred yards to the west, along the 'Sixth', is a much smaller farmhouse which is also a McRae property. Bridge End is a community in Lancaster Township, within Glengarry County.

Photo of the Brick House taken by Charlie McGee in 1938/39

Living in the Brick House in 1911 at the time of the Canadian Census (1st June) were:

Duncan Christopher ("D.C.") McRae (72)
James ("Jim") McRae (son, 30)
Margaret ("Maggie") McRae (Jim's wife, 28)
Mary McRae (daughter, 26)
Donald McRae (grandson, 5)
Anna Margaret McRae (granddaughter, 3)
Roderick McRae (grandson, 7 months)
Charles ("Charlie") Magee (grandson, son of Mary McRae & Dr. Charles Magee, 4 months)
Alfred Rosser (hired man, "laborer", arrived from Bristol (England) on 12 March 1911, 36).

Living in the small farm next door ("The West House"):

Farquhar McRae (brother of D.C., 64)
Ellen ("Helen") (sister of D.C., 73)
Annie McPeake (niece of Farquhar, 34) and her adopted daughter, Emma (5)
Olive Nolan (home child, 10)
Allan McGinnis ("laborer", 59)

Back row: Maggie, Jim (holding Emma McPeake, niece), Mary (holding Charlie), Alfred Rosser.
Front row: Chris, D.C. (holding Anna Margaret & Roddie on his knees), Donald, Olive.

Photo probably taken in May 1911 by D.C.'s sister, Helen. It was said that D.C. owned the only camera in Glengarry at that time. Most likely a Brownie Box Camera which first appeared in 1900.

D.C. was very much the patriarch of the McRaes in Glengarry. He was born in Lancaster Township and was a farmer throughout his life. He married Margaret McRae in 1876 and became Reeve that same year, serving until 1879. He became Reeve again in 1885 and 1886. His wife, Margaret, died of 'consumption' in 1886 aged 41. D.C. was elected to the Counties Council again in 1897, becoming County Warden in 1898. He ran unsuccessfully as a "staunch Liberal" in the Federal Election of 1898. He was Division Court Clerk from 1887 to the time of his death in 1911. He was very active in successfully opposing a move to separate Glengarry from the United Counties in 1892. He was a key figure in the establishment of St. Margaret of Scotland Church in Glen Nevis in 1882 and was also one of the founders of the Glengarry News in 1892. For many years he served as a Justice of the Peace. In short, he was a pillar of Glengarry County, greatly admired and respected and a person with considerable influence in the Catholic and Liberal circles in Upper Canada during the years between 1870 and 1911. It is said that a young student in Catechism class, when asked who made the world, promptly responded "D.C. McRae". His obituary (29 December 1911) referred to *"his kindly personality, his genial manner and his courteous treatment of all with whom he came in contact"* and described him as *"a man of incorruptible integrity"*. His funeral was *"the largest, the most representative, seen in Glengarry for many years, close upon two hundred carriages forming the cortege, many of whom being present from Montreal, Cornwall, Ottawa, and distant points in Stormont and Glengarry"*.

D.C. McRae (on left) and Farquhar McRae (undated photo, probably 1890s)

D.C.'s younger brother Farquhar never married and lived in the West House with his sister, Helen. He also served as a Reeve for Lancaster Township in

1910-11. He was much admired as *"a man of the highest possible standing"*. Since at least 1877, his health had been poor and he had been victim of a farming accident which left him *"hunchbacked"* or *"decidedly stooped"*.

D.C had three children. Mary McRae was born on 9 September 1884. Her full baptismal name was Isabella Mary Flora McRae. She had an older brother, Alex(ander) James ("Jim") born in 1880, and a younger brother, Duncan Christopher, born in 1886. Mary was evidently a strong and determined young woman, as would be seen throughout her life. Her choice of nursing as a career was certainly a bold one and a reflection of her desire to find a life of independence away from the confining space of her home in Glengarry. Maybe she was inspired by Edith Rayside, born in South Lancaster in 1872, and the first woman from Glengarry to attend university, graduating from Queen's in 1896. She graduated as a nurse in 1901.

To the left, Water Street Hospital built in 1866.
To the right, wing erected in 1897.

So, it was maybe no coincidence that, at the age of 18 in 1902, Mary McRae registered as a student nurse in Ottawa. The d'Youville School of Nursing was established at the Ottawa (General) Water Street Hospital (corner of Bruyère and Sussex) only six years earlier, in 1896, by the Grey Nuns of the Cross *"to prepare nurses to provide humane care for patients within a*

Catholic educational milieu". On 8 June 1905, Mary was one of seven young women to graduate from the three-year nursing program. She obtained a mark of 93% in all subjects and the highest mark in surgery for which she was awarded a gold medal presented to her by Lady Laurier (wife of Sir Wilfrid Laurier). She gave the valedictory, described as *"a beautifully delivered retrospect of the three years of work and a touching farewell to the institution."* Dr. F.X. Valade gave an address, concluding that *"every young girl before getting married should follow the training as a nurse if only for a year, and if she did would acquire that patience and endurance necessary to put up with the fault-finding and grumbling of husbands"*. The irony of these words would not be lost on Mary McRae after she married Charles Magee just three years later.

Mary McRae (undated photo, probably around 1908)
She was 5' 6", with brown hair and gray eyes.

The Magees

The Magees were Wesleyan Methodists from the Cavan area near the border with Northern Ireland. Charles Magee's grandfather was a Methodist preacher. The family arrived in Canada in 1820-23 and settled on a farm just south of North Gower, about 40 km. south-west of Ottawa.

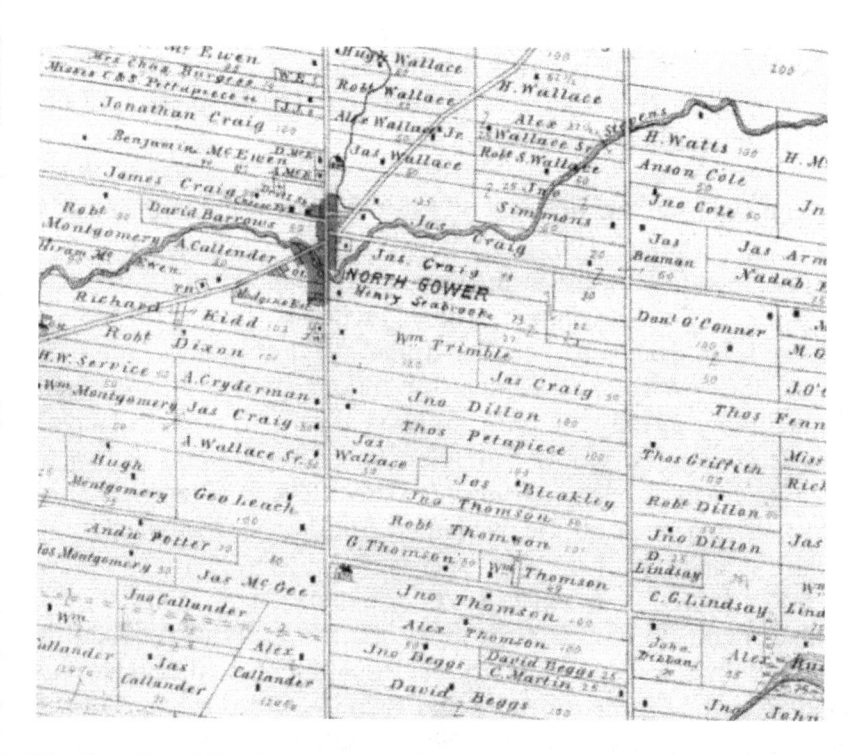

Charles Franklin Magee was born on 13 August 1875. His parents were James Magee (born 2 September 1842) and Isabella (Crawford) (born 15 October 1850). His siblings were James Malcolm ("Mack") (born 1872), Isabella (born 9 July 1885), George (died 1884), Fred (born 2 June 1895), and William (born 1880).

The precise date of Charles Magee's birth remains a question mark. To say the least, he was 'flexible' with his age. When he crossed the border into Idaho in October 1912, he gave his age as 32 instead of 37. When he enlisted

---

11

(the day before his birthday) in August 1915, he gave his age as 38 instead of 39. In the British Army, 38 was considered the upper limit for enlistment to serve overseas. Curiously, on 14 May 1927, a neighbour in North Gower (John Callander) was 'persuaded' to sign an official 'Declaration' ("in the Matter of Registering a Birth which has not been registered") confirming the date of birth as "13 August 1875". This was one year after he married Dawn Hume. On his wedding certificate (6 April 1926), he gave his age as 46. He was actually 50. When he travelled into Canada with Dawn in October 1943, he gave his age as 69 (i.e. born in 1874). In the 1881 Census, his birth date is given as 1876. In the 1901 Census it is 14 August 1874. I am inclined to believe that 13 August 1875 was the correct date, as it also appears on his application for U.S. citizenship (1 December 1927).

His father, James Magee, in the summer of 1906, following his wife's early death, aged 55, (20 November 1905), made two trips to Saskatchewan and bought a farm just outside Heward in the southeastern part of the province. Charles' sister, Bella, and their younger brother Frederick, left North Gower early in 1907 and travelled by "tourist train" to join their father in Saskatchewan. Brother William travelled by freight train bringing their livestock and machinery to the new farm. In November 1910, James Magee married Eleanor Rivington (a widow from Nepean). Eleanor went to live in Heward together with her daughter (Ellen) & sister (Ester). Ellen (Eleanor) (born 1884) worked as a nurse in the Winnipeg Children's Hospital. On 30 October 1917, she signed up for overseas service ('Overseas Military Forces of Canada'). In Ottawa, on 26 April 1920, she married an Englishman, George Warman Down (32), a Congregational "farmer". He had enlisted in 1916 and served in France as a gunner with the Royal Field Artillery. He was "mildly" wounded in the leg & foot in late 1917. He was discharged on 3 September 1919. Eleanor died on 30 July 1970 in Watford (UK).

Charles' older brother, "Mack", left home at 20 in 1892 and headed west to work on the harvest in Manitoba. Because of crop failures he travelled to Michigan, working in the lumber industry and later railroad construction. According to his sister, in 1898 he joined the thousands stampeding to the Klondike in the 'Gold Rush'. He sent few letters home and only returned to Ontario for a brief visit in 1907, unaware that his mother had died two years earlier. After a short trip to Saskatchewan, he returned to Alaska. He came back to North Gower in 1910 and looked after a farm near Stittsville for a couple of years before heading back to Alaska in 1912. He served for two years in England and France (Forestry Corps) during the Great War, returning to live near Victoria in 1919 where he had acquired a home and ten acres under the 'Soldiers Re-Establishment' program.

Charles' sister Bella studied at Victoria College (University of Toronto) and at Normal School in Regina. She became a schoolteacher in Heward, with a class of 60 (beginners to Grade VII). On 15 September 1910, she married John Wesley Gibson in Regina and moved with him to Ottawa, where their first child (James Alexander Gibson) was born on 29 January 1912. A second son (William Carleton Gibson) was born on 4 September 1913 and the family moved to Victoria (2945 Quadra St.) the following year.

Charles Magee went to high school in Kemptville and Richmond and taught for three years in the local school system in Goodstown and Munster. He went on to study medicine at McGill University, graduating in 1903. He had a summer job in 1901 selling books for commission in New York State. He completed postgraduate courses at Johns Hopkins Hospital (Baltimore) and the Society for the Lying-In Hospital (New York City). At the Johns Hopkins Hospital, Charles Magee would have studied briefly under (Sir) William Osler, a Canadian who grew up in Dundas (Ontario). Osler worked as a professor in the McGill Faculty of Medicine from 1874. In 1889, he accepted the position as the first Physician-in-Chief at the new Johns Hopkins Hospital in Baltimore, Maryland. Shortly afterwards, in 1893, Osler was instrumental in the creation of the Johns Hopkins School of Medicine and became one of the school's first professors of medicine. Osler quickly increased his reputation as a clinician, humanitarian, and teacher. At the time of his death in 1919, he was described in his obituary as *without question, the best known and best loved physician in the English-speaking world.*

Dr. Charles F. Magee (28) (1903 McGill Yearbook)
He was 5'10", with dark-brown hair and brown eyes.

In August 1904, Charles Magee acquired his first medical practice in Carp (Ontario).

Village Doctor

When Dr. Charles Magee took up his practice, the local newspaper, *The Carp Review*, described him as *"a young man of brilliant parts and [who] gives promise of a bright and useful career."* He took over the practice of Dr. W.W. Saulter who had worked there for eleven years. The population of Carp in 1904 totalled no more than 800. Charles lived on Kidd Street.

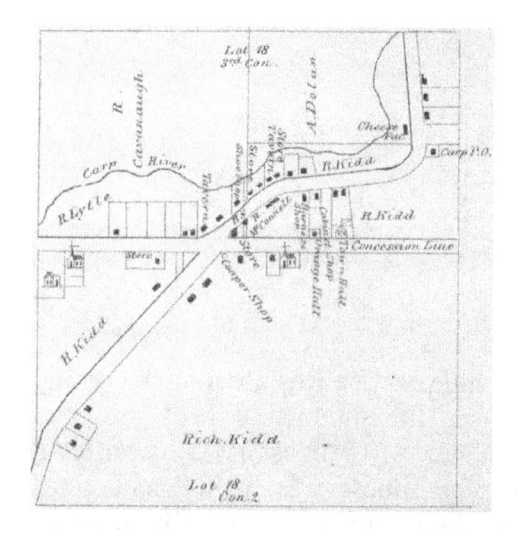

Charles quickly established himself and developed a successful practice. His presence was not, however, without controversy. He was clearly in 'competition' with Dr. George H. Groves, also a McGill graduate (1879) and certainly one of the better known and generally respected figures in Carp and throughout Carleton County. Dr. Groves was a devout Methodist and an active member of the Masonic Society. By the time Charles (30) set up in Carp in 1904, Dr. Groves (54) had been the local doctor for over twenty years.

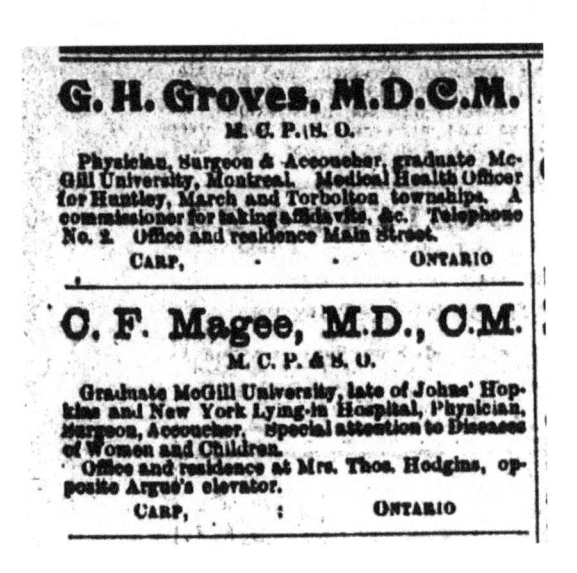

Advertisement in The Carp Review (30 March 1905)

The inevitable clash of age and professional practice was not long in coming. An outbreak of meningitis in Carp during the summer of 1905 prompted Charles to write a letter to *The Carp Review* (10 August 1905) specifically challenging the widely held view that the illness was highly contagious, requiring the imposition of quarantine on the families involved. Charles cites, among other medical authorities, William Osler, who had recently been appointed to the Regius Chair of Medecine at Oxford University. He also refers to his own experience in the Montreal General Hospital.

In a direct challenge to the approach recommended by Dr. Groves and others, Charles writes: *"It has been contended that the disease is "infectious". Some of the old school do not seem to have got proper hold of the term."* He concludes that *"shutting a family up is too serious a matter for guess work. I have found that concentration to the treatment of the cases in hand seems to give a much lower mortality than trying to impose a quarantine which, to say the least is decidedly lax."* Coincidentally (?) a small note in the adjacent social column mentions the case of Gwendoline, a little girl *"who has been dangerously ill with cerebral-spinal meningitis, [and] is recovering rapidly under the skilful treatment of Dr. McGee [sic]."*

Dr. Groves' reply was published in *The Carp Review* the following week (17 August 1905). He begins: *"Sir: — In your last issue there appeared an article signed "C.F. Magee," which I certainly would not have noticed, were it not for the fact that it contained so many statements that are utterly at variance with the facts of the case in hand, viz, Cerebro-Spinal Fever. [...] Nearly half his letter is copied verbatim from works on the practice of Medecine, going back even one hundred years, in his efforts to prove what he has certainly failed to accomplish, viz., that cerebrospinal-spinal fever is not dangerous to the Public Health."* Dr. Groves manages to find quotes from William Osler which seem to support his position that meningitis is not a "directly" infectious disease. Given the differing medical opinions as to whether the illness is "specifically" infectious or not, Dr. Groves claims that he *"ought to be allowed to give the public the benefit of the doubt [...] without being interfered with by so inexperienced a doctor as your correspondent."*

Dr. Groves rejects Charles' claim to have been the first to diagnose the disease. He says that it was he who had made the first positive diagnosis on 29 June, before Charles' first diagnosis around 16 July! Dr. Groves then proceeds to challenge Charles' affirmation that he has lost no patients to the disease: *"I am not ashamed of his insinuations that so many of my patients died, five out of 14 cases that came under my care have proved fatal. A little over 35% is not a large fatality where there are so many malignant cases, one of them being unconscious before I reached her bedside."*

Clearly sensitive about his age, Dr. Groves launches one more attack: *"His reference to "some of the old school" is so ridiculous in the premises that it deserves no reply only to state that it seems to hurt him to find that the people of Carp and vicinity have as much demand for the "old school," as they had before his advent to the village."*

The Carp Review of the following week (24 August 1905) carried Charles' response. He begins by emphasising the quality of his "teachers" to whom he attributes his "continued success". He adds that *"now my aged confrere contradicts every statement made, thus casting reflections on the highest medical authorities, hoping thereby to mislead the public and impress the idea that I disregard public health — a most unreasonable thing. In reference to his insinuations regarding my "inexperience" I wish to say it is RESULTS that count. I came to Carp one year ago confident that the intelligent public of this vicinity would appreciate the results of honest practice rather than bluffing and puffing hot air and I have not been deceived."* A few more comments about the mortality rate of Dr. Groves' patients bring Charles to his conclusion: *"Now having done what I considered my duty to the public and having no intention of stirring up a personal controversy, I refuse to recognise further, such personal harangues, entirely remote from the subject in question, as appeared in your issue of the 17th, as it is decidedly non-professional."*

Dr. Charles Magee was not one to run away from confrontation, nor would he hesitate to challenge those who held different viewpoints from his own. He was ambitious and supremely confident in his convictions. The following incident, which occurred only a few months after his arrival in Carp, suggests that he was a man of quick temper and fiery temperament.

On Saturday, 25 March 1905, two 'assault' cases were heard at the Carp Police Court. By 10:30, when the court opened in the town hall, it was *"standing room only"*. Both cases were linked, with Charles accusing Henry Lahey of striking him in the face as he came out of a local store the previous Tuesday (21st). Lahey claimed that he asked Charles why he had called him a liar the previous day and, then, fearing that Charles was going to beat him, *"struck him first"*. Although Charles was not injured, the magistrate thought *"that a lesson should be taught the young man [Lahey] and others in the community and imposed a fine of $10 and costs."*

The other case was a counter-charge and was brought by Lahey against Charles. He accused the doctor of charging too much and of taking unacceptable steps to recover the money for an unpaid bill of $50. He claimed that Charles had threatened him physically and accused him of telling lies. *"Dr. Magee in his evidence denied putting his fists up to Lahey's face, threatening to beat him or anyone else or of calling him a liar, but did accuse him of telling things about him in his practice. He said he was possibly a little ruffled at the time."* This case was dismissed with costs against the plaintiff. (*The Carp Review*, 30 March 1905)

Undeterred, Charles became part of the local community and expanded his practice. On 6 April 1905, *The Carp Review* noted that Dr. Magee *"had to resort to horseback"* to visit patients because of the muddy roads. For the Carp Fair (known then as the 'Huntley Township Exhibition'), 3-4 October 1905, the advertised prize donors included *"Dr. C.F. Magee, $5 for the best lady rider of a saddle horse; open to all, must be at least three competitors."* Just a day later (5 October1905), *The Carp Review* announced that Dr. C.F. Magee had been appointed *"Record Keeper of the local KOTM Tent"*. This referred to the Knights of the Maccabees, a quasi-secret fraternal order founded in London (Ontario) in 1878 as a primitive mutual insurance group, *"open to all white persons between 18 and 70, though those over 52 were ineligible for the beneficiary features. Applicants had to be of good moral character, bodily healthy and socially acceptable"*. Charles clearly fit right in and, as a medical doctor, had an obvious interest in health insurance, particularly when it came to payouts.

On 8 March 1906, *The Carp Review* announced that Dr. C.F. Magee had purchased the Carp drugstore, previously owned by Messrs. Graham & Elliott (*"who also have a pharmacy in Ottawa"*). The newspaper hoped for *"continued prosperity for the drugstore under its new proprietor"*.

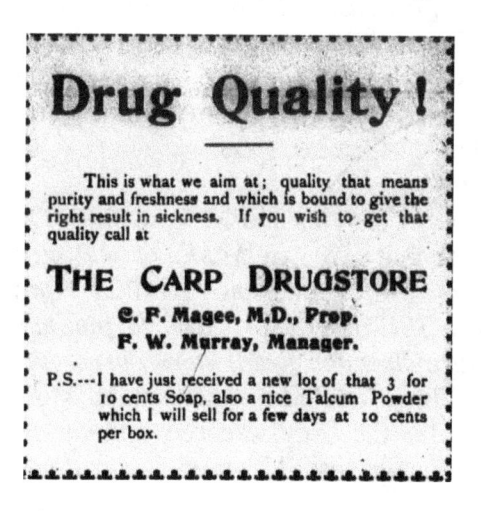

Advertisement in The Carp Review (2 August 1906).

Photo of Carp Drugstore (Kidd Block) taken between 1906 and 1911.
Dr. C.F. Magee's name appears on the sign. (Courtesy of the Huntley Township Historical Society)

With the purchase of the drugstore, Charles finished setting himself up as a successful businessman and rival to Dr. Groves. It was, however, also a difficult time for him personally. His mother's unexpected death in November 1905 and his father's plans the following year to uproot the family from North Gower and move to Saskatchewan cannot have been easy. Maybe it should be no surprise that it was about this time (late 1906) that he decided that he needed a nursing assistant. We do not know how it was that Mary McRae went to work for him, but news of her gold-medal success at the Ottawa Hospital a year earlier may well have attracted his attention. Mary McRae and Charles Magee were married on 21 October 1908.

The drugstore prospered, and no doubt so did Charles and Mary with it. On 22 April 1909, *The Carp Review* announced that *"Miss Bella McDaniel* [aged 15] *has joined the staff of the Carp Drugstore as saleslady"*. On 29 April 1909, the newspaper wrote that *"The REVIEW has been asked to publicly thank Dr. Magee for the refreshments furnished the firefighters during the progress of the fire."* A number of buildings, including the general store were destroyed on 21 April. A month later the drugstore proclaimed the opening of an *"Ice Cream Annex"*, as well as the installation of *"a new Soda Fountain"*.

Early in 1910, Charles hired William Shaw (28) to manage the drugstore for him. Shaw, whose father was a shepherd living close to Aberdeen, had arrived from Scotland in June the previous year. Before travelling to Canada, William Shaw graduated in pharmacy at Edinburgh University. He made his way first to Toronto, where he worked for six months with the Elliott Wholesale Drug Company (leaders in the pharmaceutical trade in Ontario and the west) on Front Street. The Elliott family had also owned the Carp drugstore before selling it to Charles in 1906. In Carp he lodged with Mrs Woods and her daughter on Main Street. He was a Presbyterian. On 3 February 1910 came the first local mention of *"William Shaw, M.P.S., Chemist & Druggist, Manager"*.

Over the next few months William Shaw struck up a relationship with Florence Jennings (born 1890), a domestic servant boarding with Joseph Gilchrist and family in Carp. Florence was a 'home child' who had come to Canada in 1902 (aged 11) as one of a *"special party in transit to Canada"*. Passage was paid by "Dr. B" [presumably Dr. Barnado]. The SS Colonian sailed from Liverpool on 25 September 1902, arriving in Portland (Maine) on 6 October 1902. There were about 347 in the party, most of them children ranging in age from 6 to late teens, with the majority between 8 and 12. Approximately two-thirds were boys. Around the beginning of the 20th century, about 1,000 Barnado children were being sent to Canada every year. Those over 13 were sent to farming families and worked as farm labourers or domestic servants. The younger ones were boarded out. Between 1882 and 1939, around 30,000 children travelled across the Atlantic.

According to local newspaper reports, Florence Jennings and William Shaw were engaged to be married in September 1911.

Ne Temere: marriage on the rocks

"Only those marriages are valid which are contracted before the pastor or the local Ordinary, or a priest delegated by either of these, as well as at least two witnesses ..." (Ne Temere, 1907)

The *Ne Temere* Papal decree came into general effect on Easter Sunday, 19 April 1908. It was issued on 10 August 1907 under Pope Pius X and was designed to clarify the Roman Catholic Church's stance on 'mixed' (sometimes called 'clandestine') marriages, entered into "rashly" ("temere"). The Church denied the legitimacy and validity of such marriages. It was widely interpreted as requiring that children of such marriages be brought up in the Catholic faith. Although this specific issue was not part of *Ne Temere*, it was fully and frequently covered by ecclesiastical interpretation of much earlier decrees.

The impact of *Ne Temere* was immediate, particularly in countries where there were significant Protestant populations, including Canada and Ireland. There was an instant storm of bitter controversy which raged particularly throughout the following five or six years, although it went on much longer. In May 1912, the issue of Parliament's authority to enact a Federal Marriage Act was referred to the Supreme Court of Canada. Protestant reaction was particularly strong in Ontario and it is impossible to understand the story of Mary McRae and Charles Magee without reference to this social upheaval.

We must assume that the first twelve months or so, following Mary's arrival in Carp, were relatively happy ones. She would no doubt have been lodging with a local family. In any event, Charles persuaded her to marry him. The wedding ceremony took place on Wednesday, 21 October 1908 at the Ashland Boulevard Methodist Church in Chicago, with the Rev. James Phelps officiating. It is unclear why the marriage took place in Chicago, but the city was widely known for its Methodist and Presbyterian churches. Northwestern University was founded by Methodists in 1851. By marrying quietly outside the reach of *Ne Temere*, and in a place where a mixed Protestant/Catholic marriage would raise few eyebrows, Charles and Mary may have thought they would escape disapproval or social complications.

Ironically, Charles Magee developed his own inverted Protestant vision of *Ne Temere*, demanding that Mary adopt a Methodist lifestyle. In his mind, he was convinced that any children of theirs would be brought up as good Methodists. From his perspective, the Roman Catholic faith was to have no place in their lives. In his mind, it was one of the conditions of their marriage that Mary would become a Methodist. Mary initially accepted this new challenge in her life and, in the spring of 1908, six months before their marriage, she was admitted as a member of the Dominion Methodist Church in Ottawa, by the Rev. Dr. Henderson.

For some time, she attended the Carp Methodist Church and Sunday school quite regularly, although Charles would later claim that, through the interference of priests and relatives, she became dissatisfied and wanted to return to her former faith. What is certain is that the first year of their marriage quickly showed distinct signs that all was not well and that the long-term prospects were not good. There were two powerful forces at play that would shape the events of the next few years, changing the lives of both families forever: deep-seated religious differences and the aggressive character of Charles Magee.

Charles maintained that *"the only trouble between himself and his wife [was] of a religious nature"*. At one point, he went so far as to attribute direct blame on the publication of the *Ne Temere* decree and what he called *"priestly interference"*, claiming that, from the beginning, it was Mary's intention to turn him into a Roman Catholic. Although Mary was, and remained, deeply attached to her Catholic roots, it was apparent to her, and to others, that her husband was a man of impulsive and violent nature. Her view was that most of their difficulties grew out of her husband's temper. There is evidence that, less than one year after they were married, Charles became insistent that Mary attend the Methodist Church *"or get the hell out"*.

Mary later testified that, during that first year, there had been arguments about their religious differences, saying that Charles *"was always harping about it at the table"*. Charles himself acknowledged that, on one occasion, he had compelled Mary to attend a tea meeting against her will, and said that *"she did not want to go because it was a Methodist tea meeting"*. He saw further evidence of her rejection of his faith in her attitude to the Bible, when she threw it aside saying it was *"only a concoction of King James"*.

Things came to a head when Mary insisted that they have a second wedding ceremony. In her view, and that of the Catholic Church, their marriage in Chicago was not legitimate and they were, in effect, living in sin. Mary argued that *"there were some of the teachings of the Methodist Church that were not in accord with what I thought were right"*. By late 1909, Mary refused to accompany Charles to church, urging him that they be married again by a priest.

On **20 January 1910**, Mary left Charles for the first time. Her father, D.C., travelled to Carp to fetch her, telling Charles that, unless he agreed to be married by a priest, Mary would return with him to Bridge End. This she did, staying with her family for the next month. Her feelings for Charles remained strong and she was intent on settling matters between them. She agreed that the two of them should meet and it was arranged that he would travel by train to Alexandria where she would be waiting for him. It was a bitterly cold day and, to Charles' dismay, only D.C. was waiting for him on the station platform. The two of them went to the nearby Atlantic Hotel and talked for an hour, after which D.C. left to find Mary. He returned a little later and told Charles that his only option was to see her and Father Dan Macdonald at the Bishop's Palace (about fifteen minutes' walk). Charles' response was described as *"more forcible than polite"*, but nevertheless Mary returned to him later in **February 1910**.

As a condition for her return she asked for *"liberty of conscience"*, maintaining that she bore no ill feeling against the Methodist Church. There is little to suggest that they had made any progress in resolving their fundamental differences. Charles persisted in reading aloud to her editorials on the subject of *Ne Temere* from the *Christian Guardian*, a Wesleyan Methodist journal founded in Upper Canada in 1829. It was a weekly publication, based in Toronto, and was the first religious newspaper published in Canada. Mary steadfastly refused to discuss the matter any further, saying only that she would return to Bridge End.

In **April 1910**, Mary realised that she was pregnant.

On **7 May 1910**, she left Charles for the second time and returned to her family, saying that Charles had failed to give her a horse and carriage to go to church, as he had promised. Presumably this was the only way she could travel to the local Roman Catholic Church, St. Michael's, about ten kilometres southwest of Carp Village. Instead, she took the train into Ottawa. Charles, on the other hand, claimed subsequently that efforts were being made to persuade him to renounce his faith, including unspecified offers of money and even a position in a hospital.

Two months went by and then on **5 July 1910** Mary returned once again to Charles, *"of her own accord"*. Things must have seemed relatively settled between them and they took a trip together *"all through the western states"*. The remainder of 1910 seems to have been uneventful as far as their marriage was concerned. However, her approaching due date would certainly have added further stress.

On 6 January 1911, Miss Fanny Davidson, who had been working for the Rev. Mr. Anderson in Ottawa, was engaged by telephone and came to live with Charles and Mary in Carp to help look after the baby. Charles Stewart Alexander Magee ("Charlie") was born on **11 January 1911**. His birth certificate lists him as "Chas Stewart Magee". He was baptised a few days later by the Reverend F.G. Robinson, pastor of the Carp Methodist Church.

On 8 February 1911, the *Christian Guardian,* under the headline *'Mixed Marriages',* described the woes of a Presbyterian woman in Belfast whose Roman Catholic husband deserted her and arranged the kidnapping of their two children when she rejected the demand of a priest that they be remarried in the Roman Catholic Church. It is hard not to believe that Charles was putting his own mirror-image interpretation on the whole story. The 'McCann case', as it was known, drew huge public attention and figured in a major debate in the British House of Lords on 28 February 1911. It was also a subject of intensive debate in the Canadian House of Commons in October of the same year: *"The opposition to the application in Canada of the Ne Temere decree raised an opposition which is too well known and clearly defined to need further mention."* (*Toronto Star*, 25 October 1911).

Fanny Davidson was to prove an important witness during Farquhar's trial later in 1911 stating that, on one occasion, Mary escaped downstairs with her clothes nearly torn off. She said that she had begged the doctor to leave his wife alone and heard the doctor say that he would *"trim"* his wife. She had seen the doctor knock his wife down and had also seen her nose bleeding after his attacks. The doctor had threatened to smash his wife's face. *"She had never seen a woman so badly used"*, said Fanny.

She also corroborated the statement, given in evidence by Mary, describing the events of **3 May 1911** which led Mary to leave Charles for the third and final time two days later. At breakfast that day Charles told her that she must go with him to a funeral in Marathon (about 8 kilometres away). Mary said that it was too cold, that she was unwell and that if she went she would have to leave the baby with someone. Charles replied *"that's only a whim of yours, old girl, you're going to that funeral"*, using some strong language. When Mary had finished breakfast, she went out toward the porch to see the baby. Charles sprang ahead of her, closing the door and locking it. He said it was just bigotry that kept her from going to the funeral. He then put his hands on Mary and tried to force her to go upstairs. *"I got down on the second step and took hold of the banister and called for Mrs Davidson to go for help. He told me 'not to get excited' and ordered Mrs Davidson not to pay any attention to me. He had forced me from the front door to the steps with his hands on my throat and was trying to force me upstairs. I was afraid to go. He took me by the throat again and said 'are you going to the funeral?' I replied 'no'. He said 'you will go, young lady, or I will take you there by the hair of the head or I will break your neck'. Then he used words so vile that I couldn't repeat them unless the ladies in the courtroom go out. Mrs Davidson said to him 'remember she is a woman'. He paid no attention to her."*

On **5 May 1911**, Charles attended a horse show in Ottawa and later bought *"a little collapsible go-cart for the baby"*. When he returned to Carp that evening he discovered that Mary had packed her trunks and had taken the train, along with baby Charlie, on her way back to her father's house. Two days later, on **Sunday, 7 May 1911**, Charlie was baptised in the Glen Nevis Church, St. Margaret of Scotland. Father Dan Macdonald performed a *"conditional"* baptism, noting for the record that the father was a Protestant.

[This is] the rite of baptism performed on a person who is entering the Roman Catholic Church and is not certain about previous baptism. This is not rebaptism, which is impossible, since this sacrament can be received only once. But if there is reasonable doubt about the fact or validity of one's previous baptism, the sacrament is administered conditionally, i.e., the one who performs the ritual at least mentally says, "If you are not baptized," and then proceeds to confer the sacrament. (Catholic Dictionary)

A strange court case took place in Ottawa on 29 May 1911, in which a jeweler by the name of Mr. J.E. Wilmot sued Charles for a *"$16 pearl and diamond stick pin"* taken *"by mistake"* two months previously. Charles asked his brother, Mack, to return the pin but it never arrived. Mary, called as a witness, travelled to Ottawa to attend the hearing, but she was accompanied by another woman and a 'detective' and Charles was unable to talk to her. Judgment was reserved and nothing more is known about this very bizarre business, which apparently drew a lot of interest at the time among the legal profession!

Whatever the explanation, it is certain that Charles was becoming increasingly obsessed with the idea of recovering his *"son and heir"*, with or without the mother. On **Sunday, 4 June 1911**, a day after borrowing a car from a friend in Ottawa, Charles travelled to Alexandria together with his brother, Mack, and the young Scotsman, William Shaw, who managed the Carp drugstore. They registered under assumed names and *"hired a team to drive them to Bridge End"*. Upon arrival they were confronted by D.C. who made it clear that, unless they had legal authority, they would not be permitted to see Mary or the baby.

Charles and his companions returned to Carp, but clearly the matter was far from settled. Charles subsequently wrote abusive letters to Mary (full of *"very filthy and ugly language"*), calling her *"a little papist bitch"* and threatening *"a visit from the bunch"*.

The stage was now set for the drama which took place just four weeks later.

Battle of Bridge End

Charles was convinced that, during the month of June, he was being shadowed repeatedly by men who were apparently set to watch him. It seems highly plausible given that D.C., a man with considerable influence and friends in high places, suspected that Charles might return to Bridge End, intent on causing trouble. Early on **Saturday, 1 July 1911**, D.C. received a disturbing phone call from his contacts in Ottawa. D.C. would have been one of very few people in Glengarry with a home phone, at a time when long-distance calls were still a novelty. Businesses advertising in the *Glengarry News* in 1911 rarely included a phone number and, if they did, it would be something like '3' or '25'.

That morning, Charles and William Shaw caught the morning train into Ottawa where they met Charles' brother, Mack. They made their way from Union Station to a car dealership on Sparks Street (Pink, McVeity, & Blackburn). There they hired a car, along with a chauffeur, Bert Tomkins (18), and set off for Cornwall, then on to Bainsville where they stopped to pick up a 'Special Constable' by the name of John Uren. Charles had already written to Uren to make this arrangement. The journey to Bainsville (about 140 km) would have taken approximately three hours, and they would have reached Bridge End about thirty minutes later, towards the end of the afternoon.

The car would have looked something like this. In 1912 Ottawa "boasted of over four hundred automobiles."

It was an unusually hot summer with temperatures often reaching the low thirties. July 1st was Dominion Day and Charles had calculated that the McRae men would all have gone to the horse races in Dalhousie Station, leaving the Brick House relatively unprotected. In this he was mistaken. Mary's brother, Jim, was the only member of the family who left Bridge End that day.

D.C. had seen the threatening letters from Charles and was afraid an attack was coming. When he received the telephone call that a *"fully armed"* group of men was on its way, he sent an urgent message to a local police constable asking him to come immediately to the Brick House. The constable, Kenneth McDonald, arrived around 9:30 that morning and stayed there the whole day. He was unarmed, but it was intended that he would provide protection and arrest the intruders if necessary. D.C. went over to his brother's place where Farquhar and Alfred Rosser, the hired man, were taking an early lunch intending to join Jim at the Dalhousie Station races. He said to Farquhar *"those people are coming out again, surely you will not leave us alone"*. Farquhar and Rosser both agreed to remain. His son's wife (Maggie) fainted when the telephone message was received. She and the rest of the household had been in constant fear and *"a state of terror"* for the past month. Early that afternoon, Mary took 5-month-old Charlie and found a place for them to

Mary and Charlie's hiding place. Photo of the old elm tree taken by Charlie in June 1938.

hide behind a large elm tree in a field about two hundred yards from the house.

The "bunch" arrived shortly after 5 o'clock. Charles sat beside the chauffeur, with Uren, Mack, and William Shaw in the back of the car. Accounts vary but it seems that at least two, and probably three, of the men carried revolvers. Charles was confident that *"the plan of attack was made and well carried out, every egress from the house being covered"*. He claimed later that he had obtained advice from three lawyers, all of whom had told him that he had a right to recover his child. His older brother, Mack, on the other hand, was less convinced, *"objected to the plan of campaign and advised against taking the law into [their] own hands"*. Charles subsequently acknowledged that he had taken no legal steps to recover his child and that his expeditions were contrary to law. He also admitted that he and Shaw had both been armed on the two occasions that they had gone to Bridge End.

Inside the Brick House, D.C. waited with Maggie and Constable McDonald. Maggie's six-year-old son, Donald, was also with them, but D.C. sent him over to Farquhar's house when he realised that Charles and his group had arrived. The other women and grandchildren were all with Farquhar. These included Farquhar's sister, Helen, and a visiting relative (Annie McPeake) with her five-year-old daughter, Emma.

As the car drew up, D.C. was standing near the stables on the opposite side of the road. The plan of attack was immediately put into action and, while Uren held D.C., Maggie, and Constable McDonald at gunpoint, Charles began to search for Mary and the baby. He entered the house by a side door and looked through every room upstairs and down. Meanwhile, Mack and Shaw walked up and down the road. Uren would later claim that he had no gun but that he had produced a pair of handcuffs which he always carried with him.

Having been unsuccessful inside the house, Charles proceeded to search the outbuildings and the orchard but to no avail. D.C. tried threatening Charles with a stick and then brought out his old gun, intending to scare him off. The gun was not loaded and was in fact incapable of being fired.

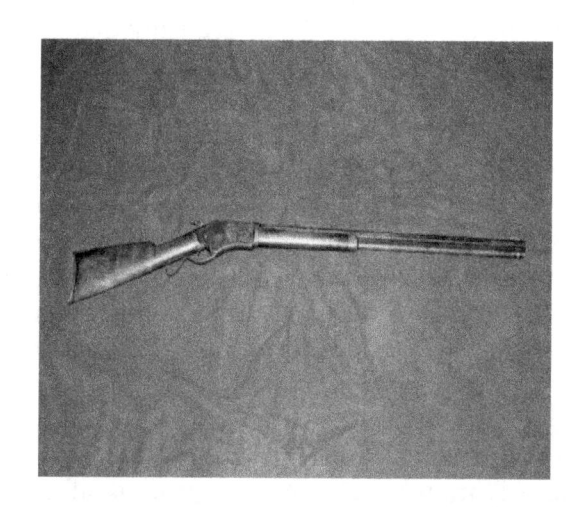

D.C.'s gun. It is a Whitneyville Armory .44cf. 28" octagon barrel, with lever action. It is a shotgun but was not loaded. It was nearly thirty years old in 1911.

Meanwhile, Farquhar and Rosser had arrived on the scene. D.C. produced an axe which he handed to Farquhar telling him to cut the car tires. Modern pneumatic tires were not yet in common usage and an axe would certainly have done considerable damage to the solid rubber tires of Charles' car. The nervous young chauffeur, Tomkins, insisted on moving the car fifty yards down the road out of harm's way, in spite of being instructed to stay where he was.

Charles, increasingly desperate, continued his search. He and Uren next appeared to be heading in the direction of the old elm tree. D.C. called out to them to go no further, saying that he had every intention of shooting. His bluff succeeded and the two men turned and cut back across the field returning to the car.

As they were about to drive away, Charles looked back and saw a woman with a child standing outside Farquhar's house. It was too far for him to see them clearly but he suspected that it might be baby Charlie. He and Uren got out of the car and headed back along the road. They were immediately confronted by Rosser who had brought out a double-barrelled shotgun belonging to Farquhar. He threatened to *"blow their bloody heads off"* and dropped to one knee as he took aim. The threat worked and, realising that the child was not his son, Charles and Uren went back to the car.

At that moment, Farquhar re-emerged from his house carrying his hunting rifle. This was a modern weapon described as *"a Marlin 44 rifle with large bore and strong carrying powers"*. Uren, not the most reliable witness, said that he heard Farquhar call out *"you damned Protestant pup"*, or words to that effect, although this was not confirmed by any other testimony. The car started off going east and was about two hundred yards away heading down the far side of a slight rise in the road. The occupants were looking back and saw Farquhar take aim.

A single shot was fired and, given the distance, it may well have ricocheted before hitting the car. The bullet passed through the cushion or padding of the back seat just above the woodwork. It went through five or six folds of the cover of the automobile, which was down at the back at the time, and also through one of the oak rims framing the top. The bullet entered William Shaw's back below the left shoulder, breaking two ribs, and piercing his left lung. Charles maintained that the bullet was meant for him and that he only survived thanks to a jolt as the car hit a small rut or stone, changing the course of the bullet.

They drove immediately to the office of Dr. Faulkner in Lancaster, a distance of 25 kilometres, where the wound was dressed and where Charles administered a morphine injection. They then took Shaw on the 20:30 train to the hospital in Cornwall, where the doctors had very little hope that he would recover. Shaw never lost consciousness during any part of the journey, and he seemed to be doing as well as could be expected.

Neither Farquhar nor anyone else at the Brick House had the slightest idea that somebody had been wounded. They assumed that they had successfully repelled a violent attack and that, for the time being, Mary and Charlie were safe.

So it was with considerable surprise and shock that, coming out of mass at St. Margaret of Scotland in Glen Nevis on Sunday morning, the family was confronted by Constable Smyth of Cornwall, in the company of the selfsame Constable Uren. They had a warrant to arrest Farquhar and took him to Cornwall where he was charged with *"shooting with intent to do serious bodily harm"*.

The Carp Review commented already on 6 July 1911: "We *fear the doctor is not taking the proper steps to secure his child. It is a sad affair from every point of view – a home broken up, husband, wife and child parted, a disinterested young man who was just about to be married lying on what may yet prove to be his death bed, a grief-stricken bride-to-be and a respectable farmer in jail awaiting his trial on a very serious charge."*

Shaw's condition did indeed deteriorate and, on 6 July, lawyer Robert A. Pringle was called to the hospital late at night by the Coroner Charles Hamilton to witness an 'antemortem statement' from the dying man. The statement read as follows: *"I saw a man come out of the house with a gun, I believe him to have been Farquhar McRae. I saw him take aim and fire. The shot or bullet passed through the top of the seat and struck me just below the angle of left shoulder blade. The man who fired the shot came out of the house opposite D.C. McRae's."*

Farquhar appeared before Police Magistrate Daniel Danis for a preliminary hearing on the morning of Friday, 7 July 1911. Charles had failed to turn up (*"owing to the poor railway connections"*) in spite of a telegraph message requesting him to attend. The Crown Attorney (James Dingwall) was displeased by the way the 'antemortem' statement had been taken without him being present. He was not willing to proceed, particularly in light of a note written by Dr. Aguire of the Cornwall Hospital saying that Shaw's condition was worse and that he was not expected to live more than twenty-four hours. Counsel for Farquhar (R.A. Pringle, K.C. and J.A. Chisholm) did not object to an adjournment and requested that their client be released on bail of up to $15,000. In spite of Farquhar's age and his outstanding reputation in the community, in spite of the fact that he was a Reeve of Lancaster Township, and in spite of sureties guaranteed by D.C. as well as the local Conservative MPP Donald R. McDonald and *"other prominent Glengarrians"*, a decision on bail was postponed and the hearing was adjourned for seven days.

Following the adjournment of the preliminary hearing on Friday, 7 July, news came that Shaw had passed away late in the afternoon. Dr. Charles Hamilton immediately made arrangements for a coroner's inquest and an eleven-man jury was selected. That same evening at 8:00 pm, the members of the jury went to the hospital where they viewed the victim's body. The inquest was then adjourned to Thursday, 13 July 1911.

When the inquest resumed at 10:00 am on the 13th, the jury was able to inspect the bullet hole and damage to the car, which had been brought to the court in Cornwall from Ottawa. A new top had been installed. Evidence was provided by Tomkins, Charles, Mack, Uren, Rosser, and D.C.. Uren came in for severe criticism for *"assisting in an unlawful expedition and trespassing on the McRae property"*. He seemed to think that because he went as a friend, instead of in his official capacity, he had not acted improperly. A threatening letter from Charles to Mary was introduced as evidence, but, because of the *"foul language"* it contained, the Coroner *"asked the ladies to retire while it was being read"*. It was not in fact read out in court but was handed to the jury. Evidence on the results of the postmortem was provided by Dr. Duncan Alguire and Dr. Charles Magee.

After a full-day's hearing, the jury reached its verdict: *"We, the jury, empanelled to find when, where, how and by what means Wm. Shaw came to his death, do, upon oath, say that William Shaw came to his death from a bullet fired from a rifle in the hands of Farquhar McRae, at Bridge End, county of Glengarry, first day of July, 1911, the said William Shaw dying from the effects of the wound at Cornwall, July 7."*

A verdict produced by an inquest jury is not a verdict of guilt but rather a determination of the cause of death, possibly including an "allegation". The file is then transmitted to the police for prosecution at a preliminary hearing. In this case, a "true bill" was brought by the jury indicating that a majority were convinced that there was enough evidence to lay formal changes.

Police Magistrate Danis resumed the preliminary hearing next day (Friday, 14 July 1911). The charge had been changed to one of "murder". Farquhar was present in the courtroom and pleaded not guilty. The evidence was essentially the same as that given at the inquest. It emerged, however, that

Uren had driven with Charles from Bainsville to Bridge End on a previous occasion. D.C. testified that the distance to the car from where the shot was fired was close to 300 yards. Of some interest was a second letter written by Charles to Mary sometime in June. It read: *"Tell Jim to go way back [...] and you do the same, but be sure you have a body guard, or you will be stolen."* Dr. Hamilton read Shaw's 'antemortem' statement to the court and R.A. Pringle, K.C., indicated that none of the defense evidence would be presented at this time. The hearing continued at 10:30 am on Saturday, 15 July 1911, and concluded just before noon with Farquhar's committal for trial.

Police Magistrate Danis expressed regret at this outcome and said that he would have preferred a reduced charge of "manslaughter". The Crown, however, was determined to find Farquhar guilty of murder and would not consider such an option. Magistrate Danis described the actions by Charles and his party as *"shameful and insulting in the extreme"*, and said that he would have considered a response by the McRaes as fully justified. However, the fatal shot had been fired only after the Magees were already leaving, making the crime appear to be one of deliberate intent. Farquhar was returned to prison in Cornwall to await his trial for the murder of William Shaw.

On Saturday, 8 July 1911, William Shaw's body was sent by train to Carp for burial. Hundreds paid their respects as they visited the open casket in Charles Magee's parlour. The *Ottawa Journal* noted some sprigs of white heather which had been placed on his breast *"often the token of a Highland betrothal"*. The reference to Shaw's planned wedding to Florence Jennings a few weeks later was unmistakable.

William Shaw's funeral took place next day (Sunday) in the Carp Presbyterian Church. The service was conducted by the minister, the Rev. P.F. Langill, and was attended by over 200 people. The 'Dead March' from Handel's *Saul* was played on the organ, prayers were offered seeking *"mercy for those responsible for the untimely end of this young man"*, and the minister preached his sermon on the theme *"What is your life?"*

Life sentence

Cornwall Court House and Jail (1909)

Farquhar was held in the Cornwall County Jail until his trial began on 24 October 1911. Inevitably, there was huge public interest and there were so many people from out of town that the hotels were full. There were even cots in the corridors and a great number of people were simply unable to find accommodation

The Honourable Mr. Justice Robert Sutherland

The Fall Assizes opened in Cornwall on Tuesday afternoon (24 October 1911) with Justice Sutherland presiding. It recorded the formal arraignment of Farquhar along with his plea of 'not guilty'. One journalist described Farquhar as *"decidedly stooped, with a heavy brown beard and thick black hair, wearing a black suit"*.

The Hon. Robert Franklin Sutherland was a justice of the Supreme Court of Ontario who had previously served as Speaker of the House of Commons (1905-1908). In 1900, he had been accused of being a member of the anti-Catholic Protestant Protective Association. Although he denied this, he admitted to having attended one of their meetings *"out of curiosity"*. Justice Sutherland was of Scottish-Irish parentage, was a devout Presbyterian, and an indefatigable cricket player. He began his career as a small-town lawyer in Windsor, Ontario. He was elected as Liberal M.P. for Essex North in 1900 (and again in 1904 and 1908) and remained in the Government of Sir Wilfrid Laurier until 1908. He resigned when he was appointed a judge in the High Court division of the Supreme Court of Ontario in 1909 at the age of 52.

Selection of the jury began at 09:00 on Wednesday morning (25 October 1911). 44 men had been summoned for jury duty and, of these, 23 were dismissed following challenges by the Crown (8) and the defence (15). The twelve finally chosen were: G.D. Deruchie (Charlottenburg), Arthur N. Barkley (Williamsburg), Sidney McConnell (Osnabruck), John J. Moak (Osnabruck), Matthew Beckstead (Williamsburg), A.M. Dixon (Matilda), Sandy Kennedy (Kenyon Township), W. McIntosh (Cornwall), Charles E. Keeler (Iroquois), Arthur McConnell (Osnabruck), W. Clayton (Cornwall), and James Farmer (Winchester).

Contemporary census information tells us that 9 of these were Protestant (6 Presbyterian, 2 Methodist, and 1 Lutheran) and the 3 others were Roman Catholics. While it is impossible to determine whether the outcome of Farquhar's trial was prejudiced in any way as a result of the composition of the jury, it is easy to understand popular hostile reaction to the guilty verdict.

The Crown Prosecutor was George Tate Blackstock, K.C. (Toronto), assisted by the United Counties Crown Attorney, James Dingwall. Appearing on behalf of Farquhar McRae were Robert A. Pringle, K.C. (Cornwall), John A. Chisholm (Cornwall) and Irwin Hilliard, K.C. (Morrisburg).

Following jury selection, the Crown Prosecutor made his opening statement. He outlined the history of the case, including reference to the religious dissensions between Charles and Mary. He described how she had left her husband, taking the child with her. He made a point of mentioning the revolvers carried by Charles and others in his party, emphasising that they were *"only for defence"*. He underlined the fact that Farquhar had knelt down in order to take aim at Charles. He concluded by telling the members of the jury that it was not their business to deal with the marital difficulties which, he underlined, had nothing to do with the shooting of William Shaw.

Essentially, George Blackstock was trying to make sure that the dramatic testimony relating to the Catholic/Protestant tensions and the *Ne Temere* controversy did not divert the jury's attention away from the core of the case. He knew that some of what he considered incidental events would shock and possibly predispose the jury in Farquhar's favour. For the Crown, the key focus was to be on the deliberate intention of the accused to shoot and kill Charles Magee.

Charles Magee was the first witness called. He described the events leading to the shooting of 1st July and spoke of the state of the marriage and the religious differences between him and his wife. Under cross examination by Robert Pringle, Charles admitted to some of his ill-treatment of Mary and to having called her *"foul names"*. Mr. Pringle then introduced into evidence threatening letters which Charles had sent to Mary between May and June of that same year. Mr. Blackstock objected, appealing to the Judge to rule them inadmissible. Justice Sutherland, however, reminded Blackstock that he himself had raised the whole matter of religion in his opening statement and that consequently the letters were indeed admissible. There was quite a sensation in the courtroom when Charles was forced to admit to having written the letters and, in particular, to calling her *"a little papist bitch"*. Charles stated that he had never met Farquhar before 1st July, although he had been to his house previously. He mentioned that, on one occasion, a medical colleague had visited him and his wife in Carp and that the colleague was of the opinion that Mary was *"a victim of religious mania"*. Charles said he had done nothing to dissuade him of this view. Throughout his testimony, he attempted to portray himself as having been consistently provoked, and having every right to take possession of his son.

Mack Magee testified that he saw Farquhar kneel and take aim before firing his rifle. Cross-examined by Mr. Pringle, he acknowledged that he had *"knocked about America"* for 17 years and that, when he returned to visit his brother in Carp, he had told Miss Davidson that *"he was sorry he had come"* and that he had never before seen anything like the situation he found. He told the court that *"it was understood that the child was to be captured if anyone attempted to leave by any of the doors of the house"*.

John Uren claimed that he heard Farquhar call out *"you damned Protestant pup"* just before he fired. Under cross examination, he admitted that they had no legal authority to enter D.C.'s house and said that he knew the plan was to kidnap the child. He denied pulling out a revolver, insisting that he only had a pair of handcuffs. He heard Maggie McRae say *"Look out, he has a revolver"* and thought it was as well to let them think he had a revolver and pulled the handcuffs out of his pocket. He admitted that he was *"a boy from a home in England"*, the unspoken implication being that he was of dubious character! The evidence he gave was at times different from things he had said at the July preliminary trial and overall *"made anything but a good impression"*.

Evidence from **Bert Tomkins** confirmed that he had moved the car about 100 yards down the road to the east when threatened with an axe. The car was moving downhill when the shot was fired. Mr. Blackstock asked **Alfred Rosser** whether Farquhar took aim, but the Judge disallowed the question, agreeing with Mr. Pringle's objection that it was *"a non-legal question"*. He said that they had fetched their guns in order to protect the women. He was unable to say whether Farquhar was actually kneeling or whether he just appeared to be because of his deformity. **Dr. Duncan Alguire**, just elected as a Conservative M.P. in September 1911, had conducted the postmortem examination with **Dr. W.A. Munro** during which they recovered the fatal bullet. The Coroner, **Dr. Charles Hamilton**, testified about William Shaw's antemortem statement and also the cause of his death.

Captain Runions, a retired military officer, was called to give expert evidence regarding Farquhar's rifle and the bullet that had been fired. Mr. Pringle's cross-examination revealed one of his lines of defence. He was able to establish that the rifle was sighted at about 100 yards and that, if aimed at a person 300 yards away, the bullet would have probably gone into the ground or would have ricocheted.

The first defence witness was **John White**, a boy living not far from the Brick House. He said that, the day after the shooting, he was walking down the hill near the McRaes and about ten feet from the top he saw a stone with the mark of lead on it. When asked by Mr. Blackstock how far, he answered *"twenty feet"*. There were no further questions.

D.C. testified that he had been pushed by Charles Magee and also that Uren had drawn his revolver. In answer to questions by Mr. Pringle, he denied having interfered between Mary and Charles and said that he had, at least once, encouraged her to stay with her husband and *"try to live in peace and harmony"*. In response to the Judge, he said that he was standing between Farquhar and the car when the shot was fired.

Mary McRae told the court that an Ottawa lawyer, A.E. Fripp, had advised her to leave Charles. Mr. Blackstock again objected to the excessive testimony about the religious troubles, but Mr. Pringle maintained that his purpose was to disprove Charles Magee's assertion that the only trouble between him and his wife was of a religious nature. When asked by Mr. Pringle whether Charles had ever struck her with his fist, she replied *"Well, if he didn't, he many times put his closed fist in my face and many times struck me with his open hand."* Although Charles had sworn that no operation had been performed on her, she said that there had or, at least she had been under an anesthetic, and she supposed she was operated on. She denied telling Charles that without a second marriage ceremony she would consider that she was living in adultery.

Fanny Davidson testified to the ill-treatment of Mary by her husband. She acknowledged that she had remained in Charles' employ until he moved from Carp in August 1911. She had written to Mary once but had not given any warning of Charles' visit on 1st July. **Maggie McRae**, daughter-in-law of

D.C. McRae, corroborated the evidence of D.C. as to the attack, and the drawing of a revolver by Uren. She was near Farquhar when the shot was fired and was positive that he had not used the term *"Protestant hound"* nor had aimed the rifle. The Magee party was away over the hill and only their shoulders and the back of the car were visible when the shot was fired.

Annie McPeake, who was living at the house of her uncle, at the time of the tragedy, said she saw Farquhar with a gun when the shot was fired, but she could not say whether it was her uncle or Rosser who fired. She saw Uren with his revolver drawn. **James Milden,** Civil Engineer, produced a plan of the scene of the tragedy and testified as to the distances between the several points. **Kenneth McDonald**, who occasionally acted as a county constable and who was an eye-witness of the incidents on 1st July, testified that Constable Uren produced a revolver at the time. He denied the accused went on his knees to take aim when he fired the shot. The shot, in his opinion, was not fired with any intent to hurt anybody. Shaw was struck by accident. He added that Shaw's dying statement that Farquhar took aim at him was a mistake. **Norman Desroches**, a second gun expert, expressed the opinion that accurate aim would have been impossible, given the distance between the Farquhar and the automobile. **Constable Uren** was recalled by Mr. Blackstock to deny the statement made by the defence that he had a revolver when he visited the Brick House.

Farquhar McRae was the last witness called. In clear terms he told his story refuting the charge of murder without repeating the extensive evidence already submitted regarding the automobile visit to Bridge End of Charles Magee and his party on 1st July. His counsel advised him to confine himself to those events that directly related to the tragedy. He said he thought he should put his gun away, and so that this should be done with safety, tried to take the cartridge out. He was unable to do this and so fired the gun in order to get rid of the shot. He concluded his testimony by going down on his knees to prove his claim that, if he knelt down to take aim, the deformity in his back would cause him to over-balance. Questioned by Mr. Blackstock about William Shaw's dying declaration that he saw Farquhar come out of his house with his gun, take aim, and fire, the accused said it would not have been possible for anyone to see from the automobile if he came out of his house, because the view was obstructed by trees.

At 09:00 on Friday morning (27 October 1911), **Robert Pringle** began his concluding address to the jury. He was convinced that they would find Farquhar not guilty, but felt the need to make a powerful plea on his behalf and against capital punishment. *"I have no apology to offer, but esteem it the highest privilege to strive for the life of my old friend, Farquhar D. McRae. God has given us life, and has surrounded that life with many beautiful things, and when we sit down to discuss taking away that life which we did not give, and which once taken we cannot restore, it is the most important and sublime thing we can be called upon to discuss. It were better that twenty guilty men should escape than that an innocent man should be punished."* Although the death penalty was not often imposed in Canada, it was a real possibility if Farquhar were found guilty of murder.

Mr. Pringle next spoke eloquently of Farquhar's character and good reputation, taking the jury *"down to this old Glengarry home"*, and then emphasising that many of the difficulties in the marriage were not all of a religious nature but the result of Charles Magee's violence. Nevertheless, all that Mary wanted was liberty of conscience, and he reminded the court that John Wesley, Martin Luther, and John Knox were all champions of religious freedom *"for which stands every Scotchman of the county of Glengarry"*. He went on: *"I would rather my arm should fall powerless than it should be raised in the name of religion, as Dr. Magee's was, against one whom I had sworn to protect."* Returning to the theme of local pride (and a certain antipathy toward Toronto), Mr. Pringle concluded: *"Let me tell my learned friend that, whatever he may do in Toronto, he can't come into the old counties of Dundas, Stormont and Glengarry, and, in the name of religion, hope for sympathy or to excite prejudice against the prisoner in the box."*

Even the **Crown Prosecutor, Mr. Blackstock**, felt the need to join in the congratulations of those who recognised the quality of Mr. Pringle's appeal, and he complimented him on *"the able manner in which he had conducted the defence."* Mr. Blackstock then addressed the jury for nearly two hours, saying to them at the outset: *"Do not be carried away by this religious talk. Some of you are Roman Catholics, others Methodists, others Presbyterians and one witness was a Baptist. The different denominations are well represented, but there is one thing in this case you all can unite on and that is charity and benevolence."* Referring to the introduction of the issue of religious differences in this case, he described it as *"that horrible crime of* *gathering up and emptying the sewer pipe of the troubles in the family."* Referring to the fact that Mary had left Charles taking their child with her, he asserted that *"she had no right to do this. She had no more right to steal his child than to put her hand in his pocket and steal his watch."* After reviewing all the evidence, he told the jury that there *"was no middle measure such as manslaughter. It was a case of murder or a case for acquittal."*

Shortly after one o'clock, **Mr. Justice Sutherland** began his charge to the jury. He pointed out that *"the law was no respector of persons and that, no matter how highly respected the prisoner might be, that could not enter into their consideration of the case."* He then proceeded to address the issue of religious prejudice and tolerance, particularly in Canada:

"In a country such as our Dominion, where the peoples came originally divided by race and creed, and where people are coming from all lands and of all creeds, it is most important that, however strong we may be in our religious beliefs, however strong may be our race prejudice, we should be tolerant of the religious and race connections of others. Under our flag, religious liberty is conceded, and in a country like this it is painful to see bigotry and prejudice enter into our national life. There is no higher task for any public man than to mitigate such difficulties as much as possible."

The Judge acknowledged the effect of these issues in the minds of the jury, either in explaining the *"excitement"* aroused in the McRaes against Dr. Magee, the resulting conduct of Mary (which might well be criticised), or the *"cruel and uncalled for"* conduct of her husband. Nevertheless, he insisted that these *"private difficulties"* had to be considered *"extraneous"*. He pointed out that *"in common law, the right to the custody of the child and the right of giving it religious instructions is vested in the husband"*, but that *"Dr. Magee was quite outside of his rights to go on the McRae premises and try to take the child by force and the McRae's had a right, if force were used to enter their property, to use sufficiently forcible means to repel them."*

A key point, Justice Sutherland emphasised, was the evidence that the car was moving away when the shot was fired. *"If the prisoner fired at the automobile recklessly, carelessly, without regard for the lives of those in the automobile, that would indicate the malice which the law says must be considered in considering a charge of murder."* He said that it was for the jury to decide whether malice had been aroused in Farquhar's mind as a result of the way Charles had treated his niece. A difficulty arose, however, because Farquhar had denied being aroused or excited. Otherwise, *"if he shot in the heat of passion, the crime might be reduced to manslaughter".*

"In connection with this case there are three courses you may take. You may find the prisoner guilty of murder, you may find him guilty of manslaughter or you can discharge him." The essential questions were whether the prisoner had a motive, the significance of the conflicting evidence that Farquhar had knelt down and taken aim, the distance away of the car, and the fact that there was nothing done by Charles and his party to justify the shooting.

"If you think on this whole evidence that the prisoner's story is true, that he had no evil intentions, you must bring in a verdict of not guilty. But if you come to the conclusion that the prisoner came there with a deadly weapon and shot deliberately or so carelessly and recklessly at Dr. Magee or the party in the automobile that one of them was killed, it was murder. If you find this, but think the act was done in the heat of passion, you can find a verdict of manslaughter."

Shortly before four o'clock, the jury retired. They returned less than two hours later and the foreman announced that they found the prisoner guilty of manslaughter. The media reported that *"the prisoner, with that true Scotch grit, showed little emotion or even a change of countenance upon hearing the verdict [...] and it was with a firm step and head erect that he returned to his quarters in the jail."*

The Judge adjourned the hearing to Saturday morning. At the outset, Mr. Pringle asked Justice Sutherland to show clemency, particularly stressing that none of this would have happened if Dr. Magee and his party had not taken the law into their own hands. He presented a petition signed by nine of the twelve jurors asking the Judge to exercise mercy. He repeated that Farquhar was *"a man of the highest possible standing [...] who was unquestionably aggravated on the fatal day"* and said that *"under all the circumstances [...] justice would be fully served if your Lordship made the sentence a light one."*

The Judge did not agree. He felt that the evidence suggested that this was a deliberate killing and that a verdict of murder could have been warranted. He believed that *"the man who committed this act, intentionally or deliberately, through bad blood and ill-feeling, committed a terrible crime."* He went on: *"I do not seek to justify the course which was taken by Dr. Magee and those associated with him when they entered the property of D.C. McRae. They acted in an unwarrantable, illegal, and high-handed manner which deserved and received reprobation."*

Mr. Justice Sutherland could see no extenuating circumstances to support leniency and proceeded to pass sentence:

"After thinking the matter over very seriously, I have come to the conclusion that the proper course for me to take is to sentence you, Farquhar D. McRae, as I now do, to be confined in Kingston Penitentiary for the remainder of your natural life."

As reported by the Glengarry News (3 November 1911): *"Farquhar McRae stood unmoved while the sentence was pronounced; then he bowed his head in meek submission, turned and, accompanied by two Court constables, walked from the dock to the cells, and another act in a tragedy which has stirred the whole country was closed".* He was transferred by train to Kingston Penitentiary on 1st November 1911, accompanied by the Governor of the Cornwall Jail, A.W. Ault, and Deputy Sheriff, Robert A. Shearer.

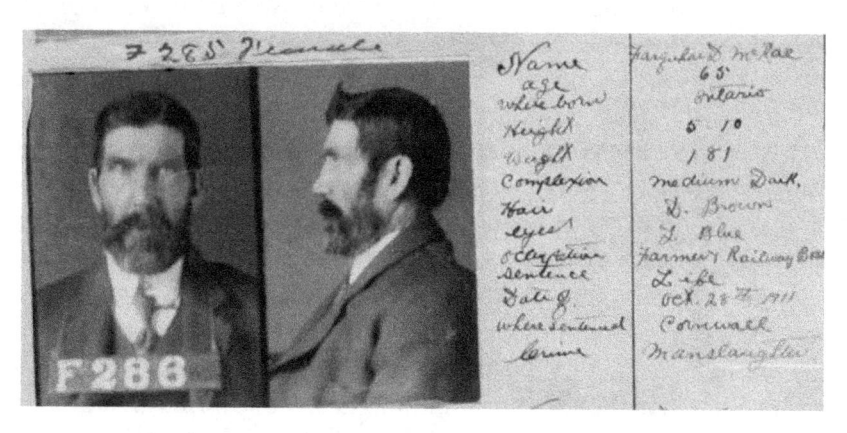

Kingston Penitentiary Inmate Ledger (Farquhar McRae, November 1911)

"The sympathy for Farquhar McRae and his connection which has been so evident, not only in his own native township, but throughout the United Counties, will certainly be intensified by the severity of his sentence, and we have no doubt when, later on, petitions praying the Minister of Justice to lighten his sentence, if not to accord him his liberty, regardless of creed or nationality, will be signed to a man."

Many people felt that this sentence was disproportionately harsh and had great concern because of Farquhar's age (he had just turned 65) and the fact that he was already in poor health. He had been receiving medical attention on a regular basis during his three months in Cornwall Jail. Reaction was fast and inevitably focused on the religious dimensions of the whole affair. On 7 November 1911, the *Canadian Freeman,* a Catholic bulletin published in Kingston had the following comment: *"The life sentence was something out of the ordinary under the circumstances connected with the case, and Justice Sutherland's ideas may become a matter of question later on. However, Catholics who are traveling towards the mixed marriage destiny should seriously reflect and think of the unfortunate outcome of the marriage of a Carp doctor to the daughter of one of Glengarry's most highly respected Scotch Catholics. Farquhar McRae's life sentence at his age of 66 was surely a surprise."*

In a similar vein, the *Catholic Register* (9 November 1911) wrote: *"The keeping of him in jail can serve no good purpose. It is one of the consequences of legal process, but we know that none more generously than his Protestant neighbors will believe him innocent and ask for his release, and we believe the authorities will not permit him to be confined long. He has suffered already, greatly suffered as a result of the man Magee's business; his niece, whom Magee claimed as his wife and treated as a dog, will suffer all her life for it, and the whole peaceful, law-abiding, God-fearing settlement has been shocked by it beyond measure."*

The impact on the entire community of Glengarry County (and far beyond) was enormous. Collective memories linger on to this day. We know little of the conditions in Kingston Penitentiary, although those who have looked at the regulations in force during the latter years of the 19th century make it clear that conditions were harsh. Food was minimal, with much the same diet served every day. The fact that Farquhar was unwell probably saved him somewhat from the most inhumane aspects of prison life, when breaking stones in the prison quarry, severe discipline from disgruntled guards, and general depression were standard realities. He was taken directly to the prison hospital department and was spared the worst.

Farquhar's older brother, D.C., must have been heartbroken. He died less than two months later on 23 December 1911 aged 72. A local obituary suggested that *"recent distressing circumstances"* had hastened his death. Official cause of death was diabetes and he died after being in a coma for four days. In his will, D.C. stipulated that *"if my daughter Mary Isabel Magee does not have any further connection or living with Dr. Charles F. McGee [!], I give and devise unto her, six shares of stock now held by me in the International Cement Co. of Spokane. In the event of her having any further connection or living with Dr. C.F. Magee, said six shares to revert to my son Alexander James McRae."*

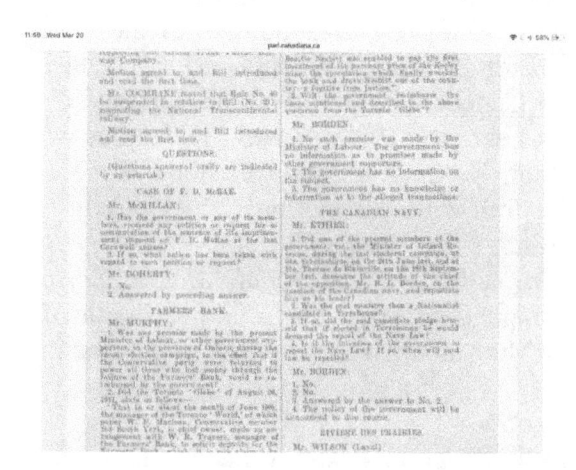

House of Commons: Debates (Hansard), 4 December 1911

A petition for Farquhar's release, or at least a reduction in his sentence, was circulating in early May 1912, to be presented to the Minister of Justice. Two questions relating to possible petitions were already raised in the House of Commons on 4 December 1911 by John Angus McMillan (Liberal M.P for Glengarry, 1908-1917): *"1. Has the government or any of its members,* received any petition or request for a commutation of the sentence of life imprisonment imposed on F.D. McRae at the last Cornwall assizes? 2. If so, what action has been taken with regard to such petition or request?" The reply from the Minister of Justice was a brief: "No". The Rt. Hon. Charles Joseph Doherty served as Minister of Justice in Sir Robert Borden's Conservative Government following the election of 21 September 1911.

It was widely understood that Farquhar's health had further deteriorated and there were real fears that he might soon die in prison. These concerns were so strongly expressed that, in early May 1912, the Minister of Justice appointed two doctors to examine Farquhar. Dr. Lafleur of Montreal travelled to Kingston Penitentiary where, together with the prison surgeon, Dr. Daniel Phelan, he carried out an examination of the prisoner. Their report confirmed everyone's worst fears and it is certain that this information contributed to the Minister of Justice's decision to release Farquhar.

Further support undoubtedly came from the Honourable Mr. Justice James Maclennan. Called to the bar in 1857, he practised law in Hamilton for two years before moving to Toronto. In 1888 he was appointed to the Ontario Court of Appeal, a position he held for 17 years. On October 5, 1905, he was appointed to the Supreme Court of Canada. He served on the Supreme Court for three years and retired on 13 February 1909. James Maclennan was a close friend of D.C. McRae's father. He gave a book ("History of the Clan Macrae", 1899) to D.C., with the following inscription: *"Presented to Mr. Duncan C. McRae by James Maclennan, Justice of Appeal, in grateful remembrance of the friendship of his father, the late Donald McRae. Toronto, March 23rd 1900."* The book remained in Mary McGee's possession. It is almost certain that Justice James Maclennan was very helpful in obtaining Farquhar's early release.

Farquhar was released on 29 June 1912, almost exactly 12 months since the day of the shooting. His nephew, Jim, travelled to Kingston and, together, they went to Jim & Maggie's house near Cornwall where Mary was also staying. Curiously, Jim was quoted in the Ottawa Journal as saying that *"the family is quite willing to call quits in the affair and let Dr. Magee, who is in Toronto, keep the child"*. There is no evidence that this was true. Farquhar lived his remaining six years in quiet retirement at his home in Bridge End. He died on 2 March 1918.

*Kingston Penitentiary Remission Register showing that, to the end of May 1912,
Farquhar had served 156 days and had earned 30 3/5 days of remission [!].*

Kidnapped

Charles Magee was not one to give in. He determined that he would get Charlie back one way or another. He very quickly sold his drugstore and practice to Dr. Osler M. Groves, of Kinburn. It was reported on 27 July 1911 that Dr. Groves would move to Carp in a few days and start his practice on 7 August 1911. Dr. Magee would remain a few weeks longer straightening out his business. Dr. Osler Groves was the son of Charles' old nemesis, Dr. George Groves, although it was publicly emphasised that father and son would not be working together and that the public would benefit from the competition.

Meanwhile rumours began circulating in November 1911 that William Shaw, who was about to be married to Florence Jennings, was already married. One newspaper reported that he had a wife in England whom he had not seen for two years. True or not, William Shaw was soon forgotten. There is no record available of his actual grave site.

On 27 July 1911, the *Ottawa Journal,* under the headline *"Is Driven from Canada by Sad Circumstances",* reported that Dr. Magee was sailing to Europe on 1 September 1911, following the *"disruption of his family through the alleged operation of the Ne Temere decree".* In addition to taking a post-graduate course in medicine and surgery, it was said to be Dr. Magee's intention to visit William Shaw's parents in Scotland. Charles' friends are quoted as believing that he might never return to Canada, or at least not to Carp, *"where he has been a prominent and practising physician and surgeon for nearly a score of years".* This 'inflation' of seven years to twenty appears typical and the whole article seems to be largely a fabrication. It is conceivable that Charles himself had deliberately given this impression of his intentions. Be that as it may, Charles was available for Farquhar's trial when it opened in Cornwall on 25 October 1911.

On 6 December 1911, Charles, through his lawyers, applied to the court in Toronto (Osgoode Hall) for custody of Charlie, through a writ of *habeas corpus.* Justice Middleton, on 8 December 1911, reserved judgement for six months in the hope that an amicable agreement might be reached between Charles and Mary. In the meantime, he granted custody to Mary, requiring that Charles be permitted to see Charlie occasionally and that he contribute financially to his son's support and maintenance. They left Osgoode Hall together, with Charles carrying the baby and Mary *"carrying the doctor's grip"*.

Mary would later confirm that she did go back to her husband, but that, *"because of his threatening attitudes"*, she felt her only choice was to leave him yet again. She moved to Ottawa soon afterwards in order to make it possible for Charles to see Charlie from time to time. She was living in a rental apartment in the Northcliffe Building at the corner of Lyon and Vittoria Streets, just west of the current location of the Supreme Court of Canada (built in 1939).

Northcliffe Apartments, 41 Lyon Street, Ottawa (1912)
(Library & Archives Canada)

On Thursday, 18 April 1912, Charles came to see the baby in the afternoon and, allaying any suspicion, offered to take them all for a ride. On their return, as Mary stepped out of the buggy, Charles grabbed the child and, whipping up the horse, made off with Charlie. Mary went to the police immediately and made a formal accusation before the deputy police magistrate. A warrant was issued for Charles' arrest but he was nowhere to be found. The police searched all trains leaving Ottawa, as well as places in the city where it was thought possible he might be, but without success.

Mary retained Robert Pringle, the lawyer who had defended Farquhar, and criminal proceedings were initiated. A motion was also made in the civil courts for the custody of Charlie, as well as against Charles for contempt of court.

Although the *Titanic* hit an iceberg and sank early on the previous Monday morning (15 April 1912), accurate news of the disaster was slow in coming and it wasn't until the 16th that the full magnitude of the tragedy became apparent. Throughout that week, newspapers were full of detailed reports and information about the more than 1,500 people who died. The kidnapping of Charlie McRae drew relatively little public attention.

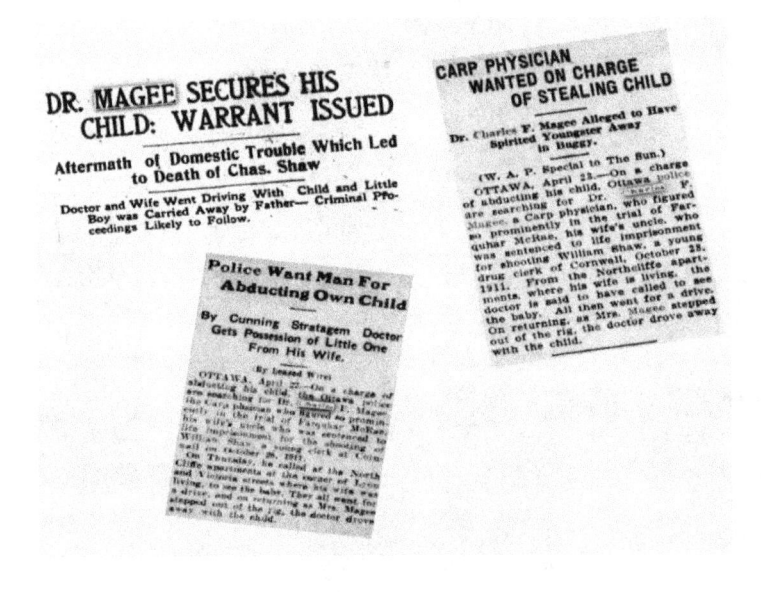

Poor Phila

On 12 June 1912, Mary appeared again before Justice Middleton in the Osgoode Hall courtroom in Toronto. She was seeking dismissal of the *habeas corpus* motion that had been brought by Charles for custody of the baby. She told the court that, after the previous hearing in December 1911, she and Charles had tried a reconciliation, but it had proved impossible. She emphasised that the baby was with Charles, that nobody knew where he was, and that he was $180 in arrears in his payments to her. She also confirmed that an arrest warrant, charging him with abduction, had been issued. Justice Middleton suggested that her only course of action was to serve Charles with notice of her motion.

Meanwhile, Charles had indeed disappeared. It is quite possible that he left the baby with his younger sister, Bella Magee, who, at that time, was living in Ottawa. She and her husband had recently moved back there from Saskatchewan. Their first child, James Alexander, was born in Ottawa on 29 January 1912. The following year, they moved to Victoria.

We will probably never know whether 15-month old Charlie was left in Bella's care for the next six months. Bella herself left a family memoir, included in a small publication in 1949 ('*The Macphersons and Magees, my kith and kin*'). References to Mary McRae are brief, incomplete, and even inaccurate. There is no mention of the Dominion Day shooting, nor of the kidnapping of 18 April 1912: "*When the baby was six months old, Isabel [Mary] took him to her home in Glengarry, resumed her profession of nursing, and never again returned to her husband.*" Other family details in her memoir are, for the most part, very precise and accurate.

What we do know is that Charles Magee travelled to Europe very soon after the kidnapping. Two months later, in June 1912, we find him in Vienna doing some post-graduate work. While shopping for a Panama hat, he made the acquaintance of the store owner, Phila Marton, a 27-year old woman born in Hungary. The two went to the races together and immediately began an intense relationship. On 22 August 1912, they became betrothed and *'exchanged rings'* in a Lutheran church in Vienna.

A week later, on 1 September 1912, Charles and Phila travelled to Innsbruck and they made their way to Canada *"in easy stages"*. They arrived in Toronto on 30 September 1912. From there, they took the train to Vancouver, and then crossed the border on 6 October 1912 from Kingsgate (BC) into Eastport (Idaho).

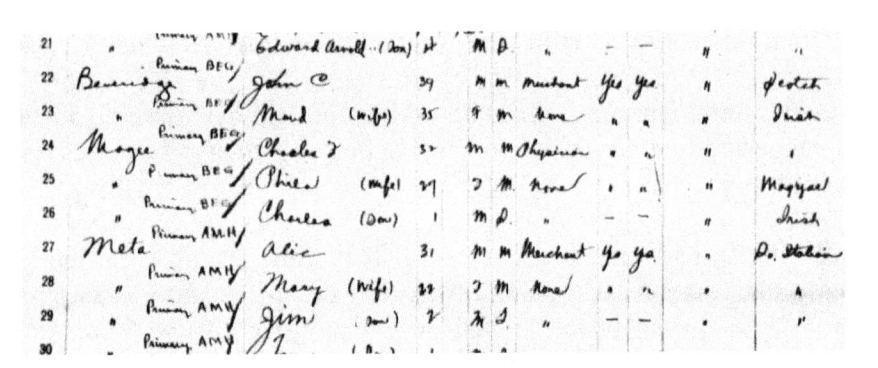

The official record of the border crossing is clear: Charles F. Magee (32), "physician"; Phila Magee (27), "wife"; and Charles Magee (1), "son". In addition to the misrepresentation of Phila as his wife, Charles also lied about his age. He was in fact 37 at the time. The biggest surprise, however, is the presence of baby Charlie. Charles had 'retrieved' his son in Ottawa and then travelled with him and Phila across Canada and into the United States, masquerading as husband and wife. Their destination was given as Spokane (Washington).

Curiously, a note in the *Carp Review* a year later (October 16, 1913) reported that *"Dr. C.F. Magee, formerly of Carp and who disappeared so suddenly a few months ago, has been living at Vienna, a city in Austria."* The note was one year out-of-date.

Charles, Phila, and Charlie seem to have remained only a few months in the States, because in 1913 they returned to Vancouver, staying first at the Windsor Hotel (52 East Hastings Street) and then moving in November 1913 to the Cedar Cottage Sanitorium (18th Avenue East), a newly opened private hospital, owned and operated by Dr. Charles Magee.

The relationship between Charles and Phila did not go smoothly, to say the least. In January 1914, Phila left Charles and moved out of the Cedar Cottage Hospital where they were living. On **29 September 1914**, she brought formal charges against Charles and they both appeared in the Vancouver Police Court. She was described as *"a tall, dark woman, with searing eyes and [wearing] a monocle"*. She apparently caused a sensation in the corridors of the Police Court by announcing to all who would listen that she is *"Mrs. Magee No. 2."* Charles was formally arraigned on a charge of *"attempting to procure an unlawful operation upon the person of Phila Marton"*.

Describing Charles as *"a man without a heart"*, Phila claimed that he had committed an illegal operation on her against her will and had performed it without anaesthetic. She claimed that Charles had then forced her to sign a piece of paper saying that she had carried out the intervention by herself. Her lawyer, Mr. Edward Bird, testified that subsequently an agreement had been reached, whereby Charles would pay her a total of $3,000 in monthly instalments, she would drop the charges against him, and would leave the country for at least five years. The payments were guaranteed through a transfer of a property mortgage. As part of this agreement, a number of documents and letters had been destroyed at Charles' request. Mr. Frank Lyons, defence lawyer for Charles, described the whole charge as one of blackmail.

According to Mr. Bird, one of the destroyed letters had said *"You will be shocked to learn that darling Phila died this morning in child birth"*. It was apparently addressed to Phila's brother, Hugo, whom Charles had met in Vienna. Mr. Bird said that only $25 had been paid and that Charles had refused to make any more payments. A building lot, worth $600 had been transferred to Phila and was considered to be a final payment on the amount agreed upon as the price of her going away and not bothering the doctor any more.

In her testimony, Phila referred to the 1st July 1911 Bridge End tragedy, describing how, in her agony following the operation, she had called to

Charles to remain with her. According to her, he just laughed and said that he was going out to the theatre. *"I have no heart. I drove beside the dead body of Shaw and then went and had a big meal after it,"* is what she alleged that he said.

The *Vancouver Daily Province* described some of Phila's early testimony at the preliminary hearing (my emphasis added):

The sensational evidence of "Madame" Phila Marton, the Austrian woman, who is bringing a charge of illegal practice against Dr. C.F. Magee, was given in a most dramatic manner in the police court this morning at the adjourned preliminary hearing. The united efforts of the court, the crown prosecutor and the counsel for the defence could not stop the flow of abuse that she heaped upon the doctor in answer to every question. She threatened to kill a man referred to during the long case repeatedly if he should come forward and give evidence of a character as suggested by Mr. Lyons, counsel for defence.

*The **famous Farquhar McRae shooting case of Glengarry, Ontario**, was referred to and several newspaper clippings having reference to the eastern tragedy were put in as exhibits, the woman having said that they were given to her by the accused when, she said, he told her that he might have to spend two years in jail. **One of the clippings was to the effect that the Magee child which had been the subject of several disputes between the father and mother following differences had mysteriously disappeared. The child, she said, was brought to her by Dr. Magee at Toronto.** "Here, Phila, is my child. Take good care of him and be a mother to him," is what she declared that the doctor said to her as he gave her the child and placed the newspaper clippings in her hand.*

After questioning the witness about her life in Vienna, where, she declared, she was the proprietor of one of the largest stores in the city, having an automobile and four servants, and relatives in the best circles of the social life of the Austrian capital, all of which, she said, she deserted to come to America with the doctor. She was asked by Mr. Lyons where she had secured the money which, she said, she had used to pay the rent of the Marton Sanitarium at 1402 Eighteenth Avenue East.

"It is none of your business," the witness declared heatedly and started to abuse the lawyer, but was stopped by the court and crown prosecutor, who again impressed upon her that she must answer as briefly as possible.

She explained, in answer to Mr. Lyons' question, at great length, the manner in which she met the doctor and several of his friends in Vienna, one of whom she characterized as a "no-good man".

Mr. Lyons – Did you hire a detective agent to look into the doctor's reputation in Canada? "No," she fairly screamed, jumping up from her seat, "I was not after his money like other people – I was not like other women." "But you did hire a detective?"

"Yes, in Vienna, I paid 400 kronin to find out about him in Vienna, and the report was good." "Do you still love the doctor?" questioned Mr. Lyons after she had told of her great love for him after their first meeting.

"Do I still love him?" she repeated with scorn, studying the lawyer through her monocle, and then springing to her feet and leaning over the table she exclaimed in a voice that could be heard outside of the closed courtroom. "I love him the same way that I love you, and I hate you. Bah." and she turned her back on her questioner.

When she was questioned as to her love for the doctor's little boy she broke down and sobbed bitterly with her head on her arms folded on the table. "Yes," she tearfully answered, and then fiercely, "and I expect to get him again some day."

Mr. Lyons – "Don't you know that his mother loves him too, and you would not want to take him away from her?"

Witness – "But he was my child too, and besides it's none of your business."

She produced a bundle of letters and documents from her muff, and demanded that they should be read aloud so that her honor might be vindicated, and the world should know of the great love that the doctor had for her. One of them was later produced as an exhibit. It was to the effect that the writer wished to see her again, and that several of his friends had declared that he had the best looking girl in Vienna. It ended with the declaration that when he saw her he would kiss her four hundred times.

It was with the greatest difficulty that she was induced to answer the questions put to her about the amount of money that she had when she came to this country. She declared that she had given the doctor $800 in Vienna to marry her, and that they had gone together to the Lutheran church there and had been formally engaged. The money was returned to her at **Toronto when** *the doctor brought his child to her and told her that she might have to earn her living for two years if he was put in jail.*

Asked if she had gone to the doctor's office after the prosecution had been laid in the Police Court, she replied that she had gone there to get bread, and had asked for $5.

"Did you want the doctor to return to you and live with you?" she was asked, and indignantly denied the statement.

Mr. Lyons – "But if a man comes here and says that he hears you do so?

"Then he is not fit for this earth, and I will kill him," she shrieked, waving her arms wildly.

The witness stated that Mrs. Magee, who had arrived from the East several weeks ago, had instigated the proceedings.

Although this last assertion is untrue, Mary had indeed arrived in Vancouver, not long after news of the preliminary hearing reached her. On **2 November 1914**, Charles went to the police to report that Mary had *"kidnapped"* Charlie. The newspapers reported that their *"six-year-old son"* had been kidnapped by his mother the evening before. Charlie was in fact only three years old. The media explanation of how it happened was that Mary, *"being on fairly friendly terms with her husband, is alleged in this way to have obtained possession of the boy."* Charles' assumption was that Mary had fled to the United States.

It is not clear how Mary returned to Toronto, but it seems most likely that she took the train. There is a family 'story' that she boarded the train with Charlie and, adopting the ruse of sitting together with a single man, was able to evade the detective who was looking for them. She was travelling with little luggage, having left her trunk behind in Vancouver.

The hearing at the assize court, before Mr. Justice Morrison, began on **19 November 1914**. Phila continued to give her evidence *"in a highly dramatic manner"*, describing herself as Charles' former lover. As she talked about their relationship in Vienna *"her voice would break and she would wipe her eyes before continuing the narrative of her alleged wrongs."*

A letter written by Charles to Phila was produced and read to the court after Charles had waived his privilege of non-disclosure. *"It was an apology for* *any wrong that the doctor might have done to the woman and stated that at one time he had honestly intended to marry her, but **owing to the fact that he could not get a divorce from his wife**, he could not do so. This letter, the witness explained, had been written by Dr. Magee, so that, in the event of any man wanting to marry the woman, she could show it to him."*

The jury deliberated for two hours but were unable to reach a decision. Charles was ordered to face a second trial and he was freed on payment of bail set at $20,000.

This second trial, with a new jury, began on **27 November 1914** and was heard before Mr. Justice Macdonald. The newspaper reported *"the presence by the side of Madam Marton of a veiled lady [which] aroused some curiosity at the trial. The lady is a well-known member of social and club circles in the city, and her presence was prompted by a kindly desire to show sisterly sympathy to the lonely foreign woman, who has been fighting for her honor and pleading her alleged wrongs before the court. Whatever is the verdict of the jury, it is probably that some of the women's societies in the city will take up Madam Marton's case and endeavor through the American consul to substantiate her story that she was lawfully married to Dr. Magee in a church at Vienna, according to the law of her native country."*

Charles' lawyer acknowledged that his client's action in marrying Phila in Vienna was indefensible and something Charles regretted. Indeed, Charles had tried to make amends by signing over his property to her. He argued that Phila must have known from the outset that Charles had a wife living in Canada. He further claimed that Charles could not have performed the alleged operation against the will of a *"tall, well built, active woman"*, and dismissed the whole story as *"absurd"*. To explain why Phila had brought the charge, he quoted Pope's famous lines, *"Heaven hath no rage like love to hatred turned, and Hell hath no fury like a woman scorned."*

Phila admitted during cross-examination that she had been jealous of Charles, even during their time together in Vienna. For his part, Charles said that Phila *"knew from the first that I was married and that it was impossible for me to marry her, yet she refused to admit the impossibility."* He claimed that her jealousy had grown even stronger in Vancouver, but denied performing any operation on her, or that she was ever pregnant. He said that he *"was never once guilty of infidelity and was never unkind to her except when once I had to lock her in the room to keep her getting out on the street and making a scene. She made life intolerable for both of us"*.

Once again, the trial lasted three days and again the jury was unable to reach a verdict. The Crown was left to determine whether to bring Charles to trial for a third time at the next assize the following year, or whether to stay proceedings and abandon the case. On **16 December 1914**, Charles' lawyer forwarded an appeal to the B.C. Attorney General to enter a stay of proceedings. Phila was referred to as *"a former housekeeper"*.

In **mid-December 1914**, Mary was already in Boston, staying with a long-time nursing friend, Anne Devanny. Mary sent the following letter to her brother and sister-in-law:

Dear Jim and Maggie – I wrote a week ago sending to Mrs. D.A. McK. [the McKinnons were close neighbours of the McRaes] and am wondering if you received it safely. Am longing for news of you all, especially Helen – and of the West if you have any. I have such terrible dreams of blood and mud and horses and Aunt Helen and Charlie and C.F. and poor Phila! Its sweet to wake and find only dreams. Did my trunk arrive or did the vile wretch get his hands on it. I wish I had my clothes. If it came send it through in bond from Hector's to Anne M. Devanny, 61 E Concord St. Boston and let her know if you send it. I expect to be at work Jan 2nd but not sure just what kind – hard to know what is best. Saw World [Vancouver Daily World] of Dec. 2. & 8. saying case goes over to Spring with the possibility of appeal to Attorney-General. You see how guilty he is when there was a 2nd disagreement. Funny we did not hear when 1st trial was on. I wish you could send me Province [Vancouver Daily Province] clippings if you have them as World is all in his favor. Poor Phila! I am very well but anxious to get to work and wish I had my trunk. I am not sure how long it will be before I get permanently settled but it will not be long I am sure as Miss Beard is very good to me – Write to me soon or to Anne. Love and all good wishes for Christmas. Love to F.D. & to Helen and the children – God bless them!

Dear Jim and Maggie I wrote a week ago sending to Mrs. Wa-
rick and am wondering if you received it safely Am longing for
news of you all especially Helen. and of the West if you have
any. I have such terrible dreams of blood and mud and
horses and Aunt Helen and Charlie and C.T. and poor
Phila. It's sweet to wake and find only dreams. Did my trunk
arrive or did the Bell-watch get per rounds on it. I wish I had my clothes.
If it came send it through from Weccars to Anna M. Devanny, 63
Georgy St. Boston and let her know if you send it. I expect to be at
work Jan 2d but not sure just what kind — hard to know what is best.
Saw World of Dec. 2 & 8. saying case goes over to Spring with
the possibility of appeal to Attorney-General. You see
how guilty he is when there was a 2nd disagreement.
Funny we did not hear when 1st trial was on.
I wish you could send me Province clippings. if you
have some as World is all in his favor. Poor Phila!
I am very well but anxious to get to work and wish I had my
trunk. I am not sure how long it will be before I get
permanently settled but it will not be long I am sure
as Miss Beard is very good to me. to Anne
                    Write to me soon, how and all good wishes
for Christmas. Love to F.D. & Helen and the children. God
bless them! Mary.

Letter from Mary to her brother, Jim, and sister-in-law, Maggie.
It is undated, but must have been written in mid-December 1914.

Mary, perhaps wisely, does not reveal that she now has Charlie with her. The mention of "poor Phila" leaves no doubt as to Mary's feelings towards Charles, the "vile wretch" who, she feared, had got his hands on the trunk she left behind in Vancouver. Anne Devanny was born in Galway, Ireland, on 20 March 1875. She came to the USA in 1892, returned to Ireland, and came back to the States in October 1903. In 1920 she gave notice of her intention to become a US citizen. She was a "registered graduate nurse" and, although about ten years older than Mary, they may well have got to know each other through the nursing programme in Ottawa. In 1917, she was supervisor of a branch station of the Instructive District Nursing Association. Mary Beard was a director of the Instructive Visiting Nurses Association of Boston and certainly helped Mary get a job working for the Visiting Nurses Association in Brockton (just outside Boston).

On **24 March 1915**, a lawsuit for return of property, brought by Charles against Phila, was heard in the B.C Supreme Court in Vancouver. Phila was not called to give evidence, but Charles argued, unsuccessfully, that he had been coerced by Phila and her lawyer into signing over the property. Mr. Justice Clement stated that, on the basis of Charles' own evidence, he found that Phila was "properly in possession of the property which Dr. Magee claimed". Phila thus retained ownership of the property and Charles was ordered to pay the costs of the unsuccessful suit.

At the opening of the spring assizes, on **3 May 1915**, the Crown announced that, because of the two unsuccessful attempts to obtain a conviction, the charges against Charles had been dropped. The $20,000 bail bonds, on which he had been held, were cancelled by Mr. Justice Murphy.

On **12 August 1915** Charles signed up to join the Canadian Overseas Expeditionary Force serving in Europe.

ATTESTATION PAPER

CANADIAN OVER-SEAS EXPEDITIONARY FORCE

QUESTIONS TO BE PUT BEFORE ATTESTATION.

1. What is your name? — Magee, Charles Franklin
2. In what Town, Township, or Parish, and in what Country were you born? — North Gower, Ontario.
3. What is the name of your next-of-kin? — Mrs. Della Magee
4. What is the address of your next-of-kin? — Manuel
5. What is the date of your birth? — August 13th., 1876.
6. What is your trade or calling? — Doctor.
7. Are you married? — Yes.
8. Are you willing to be vaccinated or re-vaccinated and inoculated? — Yes.
9. Do you now belong to the Active Militia? — No.
10. Have you ever served in any Military Force? — 11th Irish Fusiliers. 1½ years
11. Do you understand the nature and terms of your engagement? — Yes.
12. Are you willing to be attested to serve in the CANADIAN OVER-SEAS EXPEDITIONARY FORCE? — Yes.

DECLARATION TO BE MADE BY MAN ON ATTESTATION.

Date. August 12th., 1915.

OATH TO BE TAKEN BY MAN ON ATTESTATION.

Date. August 12th. 1915.

CERTIFICATE OF MAGISTRATE.

DESCRIPTION OF .... ON ENLISTMENT

CERTIFICATE OF MEDICAL EXAMINATION.

CERTIFICATE OF OFFICER COMMANDING UNIT

Charles Magee goes to war

Charles was keen on serving in the military. Even before the outbreak of war he volunteered with the 11th Regiment Irish Fusiliers of Canada which had been founded in Vancouver on 15 August 1913. It was an eight-company infantry regiment, totaling 440 officers and men. There was strong support in B.C. for the raising of militia, particularly in the wake of the Boer War (1899-1902), and a number of regiments and battalions were created prior to the First World War, as part of the general militarisation of Canada. These regiments were often made up of men of similar background and the Irish Fuseliers would have been a logical choice for a Magee.

Dress.—The battalion will parade in khaki full marching order. The haversack will contain tin cup, plate, knife, fork, spoon, towel, soap, hair brush and such necesasries as are required for the night on the train.

Baggage.—All ranks are required to bring in their personal baggage and kit bags to headquarters, 1620 William street, on Friday next, May 22, by 8:30 o'clock, where it will be piled by companies. Stores, equipment, extra camp supplies, etc., to be ready at the same place and time in order to be removed to the C.P.R. freight headquarters next morning. Kit bags should contain the following personal equipment: Towel, shaving requisites, boot laces, boot and metal polishes, one suit of underwear, two pairs of socks, tooth brush, clothes brush, candle, shirt (khaki preferred), and mending outfit. Men are required to have their hair cut short and in a soldierly manner pror to the Saturday parade.

Pay.—Pay and allowance for camp will be made to all non-commissioned officers and men according to the scales laid down in pay and allowance regulations, 1913.

Preparations for the annual training camp in Vernon.
(The Vancouver Sun, 19 May 1914)

Volunteers were involved in annual training sessions and Charles would have assumed that he was officer material.

Records show that, as of 4 April 1914, Charles was listed as a private in 'E' Company. He took part in the annual training camp in Vernon, B.C. from 23-28 May 1914 and received $5.00 as "drill pay". From 12-30 April 1915, Charles attended an officer-training course in Vancouver and qualified for the rank of lieutenant and captain.

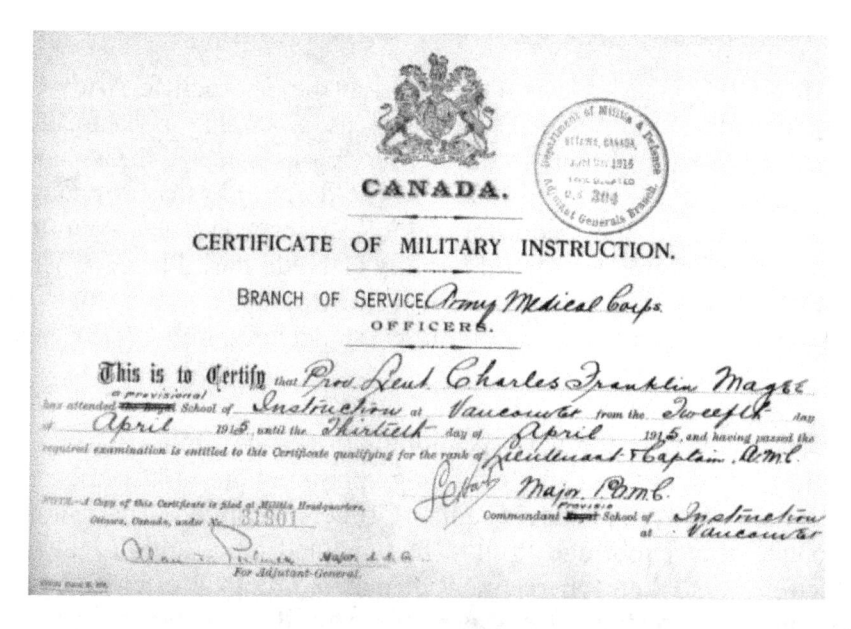

On 12 August 1915, Charles was enlisted to serve in the No. 1 Field Ambulance Depot (Canadian Army Medical Corps), with the rank of Captain.

Initially, his assigned pay was $75 a month. Payment was to be made to his brother-in-law, J.W. Gibson (2945 Quadra, Victoria), starting January 1916. The beneficiary for his army pay was given as "Mrs. Bella Magee, Dalhousie Station, Que.", described as his wife, A note, apparently from Mary's brother, Jim McRae, 20 January 1917, appeared to confirm the Dalhousie address. Bella, of course, was Charles' sister, not his wife, and she never lived in Dalhousie. There is no explanation for this curious fabrication.

In December (1915), Charles left Canada, travelling first to England before crossing to France. His arrival in France was delayed as the result of a 'quinsy' (an infection that can develop after tonsillitis). He spent nine days (2-11 January 1916) in the Canadian-run Westcliffe Eye and Ear Hospital (Folkestone). It appears that he may have travelled to France on 9 March 1916.

In early May 1916, Charles was in England at the Shorncliffe Army Camp (just outside Folkestone), which was used as a staging post for troops destined for the Western Front, as well as serving as a centre for a Canadian Training Division. On 5 May 1915, while doing physical training, he developed an infected toe, requiring minor surgery. He was sent to the Daughters of the Empire Hospital in London (1 Hyde Park Place), where the operation was carried out between 22 and 30 May 1916. On 5 June 1916, Charles appeared before a medical board which declared him *"fit for general service"*.

Charles must have spent the next six months in France, following which he was back in the Brighton area before being appointed on 30 December 1916 to serve in the recently opened Canadian Officers Hospital ('The Limes') in Crowborough, near Tunbridge Wells. He remained there until 17 February 1917, when he was taken for treatment of mastoiditis to Westcliffe Eye and Ear Hospital in Folkestone. He stayed there until 23 February 1917. He appeared before a medical board in Shorncliffe (Folkestone) on 21 February 1917, which determined that he was *"unfit for any service for 2 weeks"*, after which he would be *"fit for general service"*. A second medical board in London again reviewed his case on 27 February 1917, pronouncing Charles *"fit for general service"*. He rejoined his unit on 6 May 1917.

Once again, Charles was carrying out his duties in the war zone as a Medical Officer attached to the 44th Battalion (Manitoba). Nothing is known of the details of his service although, at various times, he was attached to the No.12 Canadian Field Ambulance, the No. 2 Canadian Casualty Clearing Station, and the No. 2 Canadian General Hospital. Field ambulance units, located near the front lines, removed casualties from dressing stations and regimental aid posts to casualty clearing stations, where urgent surgery was performed. Patients were then transferred to general or stationery hospitals and from there to a special hospital or a convalescent hospital.

The No.12 Canadian Field Ambulance arrived in France on 12 August 1916. The Field Ambulances were mobile units (mostly horse-drawn) treating wounded soldiers at the site of a battle. *"In 1914, the personnel of a field ambulance comprised 9 medical officers, and 238 other ranks. Transport consisted of 15 riding horses and 39 draught horses. The horses and drivers were from the Army Service Corps but attached permanently to the field ambulances. There were nineteen horse-drawn vehicles, which included three ambulance wagons, three water carts, four limbered wagons, seven service wagons for technical stores and baggage, one Maltese cart and one travelling kitchen. Seven motor ambulances were also, included."*
Colonel Allan D. Scott, *History of 11 (Victoria) Field Ambulance and its predecessors* (2009).

Typical WW1 Field Ambulance unit. (Library & Archives Canada)

The No. 2 Canadian Casualty Clearing Station (C.C.S.) arrived in France on 17 September 1915 and continued its work there until 7 February 1919. It was located at Remy Farm (Sidings) in Flanders, not far from Ypres. It had a bed capacity of 500 patients, or double that number in an emergency. In the

1917 campaign alone, 30,000 casualties were brought from the nearby front lines to be treated at the No. 2 Canadian Casualty Clearing Station. Depending on need, it was also relocated to Esquelbecq and Aire-sur-la-Lys in the general area south of Calais and Dunkirk. Over 75,000 patients (sick and wounded) were treated by this unit through the course of the war. Most Casualty Clearing Stations, like this one, were constructed close to railway lines in order to facilitate the evacuation of patients to general or temporary hospitals.

The No. 2 Canadian General Hospital, following an initial period near Southampton, was transferred to Le Tréport, where a base hospital, under canvas, was established. First patients arrived 8 April 1915. These extracts from the *Record of Service*, including details from the Commanding Officers' diaries, give some idea of the physical hardship involved in setting up and running this hospital, although little of the horrors of war as seen through a medical doctor's eyes at the Front:

"On August 26th, 1915, a fire broke out and completely destroyed a 20-bed ward, all its patients being rescued without injury. The Hospital occupied a very exposed position at Le Tréport, being in the open, on the cliffs, overlooking the Atlantic. Consequently, great difficulty and worry were experienced with the canvas upon the arrival of the equinoxial gales in the Fall. Huts, to replace the tents, were in course of construction, but, badly as they were needed, the work was stopped at times by the severity of the weather. One gale, on September 29th, found 1300 serious cases in hospital and no emergency shelter in the event of a ward collapsing. On November 13th, tents were torn in shreds and the patients crowded into the unfinished huts. Rain added to the difficulty and misery and both canvas and ropes became rotten owing to the strain. Then came frost and snow, with a shortage of coal and frozen water pipes. But, by the end of the year, the huts were finished and occupied.
[...]
On December 16th, the electric light supply was cut off for 12 days owing to the shortage of coal. Up to December 31st, 1916, 28,063 patients had been admitted and there had been 163 deaths, 2/3 of 1%.
[...]

The air raid attacks on hospitals in May, 1918, caused great activity at No.2. Narrow zigzag trenches were built and huts were sandbagged. Two huge tunnels, 35 and 43 feet, respectively, below the surface, were built, by the 4th C.R. Troops. These tunnels had accommodation for 1600 people, were provided with seats and lavatories and an operating room.
[...]
Although short of staff, having a team up at the front, and a number of officers on loan to other units, I cannot under these circumstances praise too much the work done by all connected with this hospital. They have all worked with a will, putting in many extra hours on duty to take the proper and necessary care of the patients. In the surgical section, it was necessary to employ at times 5 operating teams, who worked daily until the small hours of the morning, and no cases for operation were left over until the following day."

It is impossible to know which battles Charles experienced directly during the war, but, based on the dates of his time in France, we can assume that he was close to some or all of the major fighting on the western front. This would include the **Battle of Verdun** (21 February-18 December 1916, the longest battle in the First World War), in particular the **Battle of Passchendaele,** also known as the **Third Battle of Ypres** (July-November 1917), and the first **Battle of the Somme** (March-April 1918).

Wounded Canadians (1917) (Canadian War Museum)

For Charles the war ended early. Dominion Day (1 July) marked the beginning of a two-week period of rest and training. Track and field events, soccer, and baseball, were part of the celebrations. On 4 July 1918, while playing 'ring tennis' (quoits), he developed an inguinal hernia and two weeks later, on 20 July 1918, was sent to the British Base Hospital No. 20 in Camiers, near Le Touquet, about 50 km south of Calais. He had already experienced pain in the abdomen a year earlier after developing a severe cough. On 25 July, he returned to England, where he was admitted as a patient in the 10 Palace Green Hospital, Kensington, before being transferred to the recently opened Perkins Bull Hospital in Putney for convalescing Canadian officers.

It became apparent that he required surgery and on 1 August 1918, he was sent to the Leeds General Hospital & Infirmary in Yorkshire. On 4 August 1918, he underwent radical surgery performed by Sir Berkeley Moynihan, a noted abdominal surgeon. On 30 August 1918, he returned to Perkins Bull Hospital. He stayed there until 9 September 1918 when he was transferred to the Canadian Convalescent Officers Hospital in Matlock Bath (Derbyshire). This facility had recently opened on 5 March 1918 and was described as *"a deluxe hotel where allied officers recouped in luxury"*. He was prescribed a regime of *"daily Turkish showers"*.

On 24 September 1918, Charles appeared before a Medical Board (in the Buxton area). The Board pronounced him *"fit for home service, unfit for garrison duty for 3 months"* and *"unfit for general service for 6 months"*. As a result Charles returned to Canada and arrived in Vancouver on 18 October 1918. He was officially 'demobilised' on 9 January 1919.

Epilogues

Charles Magee

"He'll be a credit to us a'
We'll a' be proud o' Charlie"
(McGill University, 1903 Yearbook)

On his return to Canada, Charles travelled to Carp where he was persuaded to stay and re-open his medical practice. The Spanish influenza pandemic (January 1918-December 1920) was raging and Charles agreed to remain for a while. In June 1919, he was already serving as a district coroner for the Carp area.

In September 1919, Charles ran afoul of the *Ontario Temperance Act* (1916). Although prohibition was repealed at the federal level at the end of 1919, it remained in force in Ontario until 1927 when the *Liquor Control Act* was passed establishing the Liquor Control Board of Ontario (LCBO). Nonetheless, drinking in public establishments remained illegal in the province until 1934. Local communities, influenced largely by Protestant groups, frequently banned alcohol, although sale for communion or medicinal purposes was permitted. People could still acquire alcohol from doctors' offices and drugstores. In 1920 alone, Ontario doctors wrote more than 650,000 prescriptions for alcohol.

Carp was one such community, having already outlawed alcohol in 1907. On 18 September 1919, Charles was summoned to appear in the county police court on a charge of having issued too may prescriptions for liquor. He failed to appear and steps were being considered *"to cause him to attend"*. On 30 September 1919, the County Magistrate, Charles MacNab, found Charles guilty, fining him $50 and costs. This decision was immediately appealed by Charles' lawyer, Dr. Gordon Henderson.

Charles, in his defence, testified that his patient, Anthony Dolan (72), was suffering from an incurable disease and that alcohol was the most desirable thing to be prescribed *"for the well-being"* of the patient. Evidence was produced showing that Charles had issued eight prescriptions over a three-week period. Charles said that Dolan was *"suffering intensely and that alcohol seemed to sooth him and put him to sleep"*. Other medication could not be used because they would cause *"complications or undesirable conditions"*. A nurse, Miss Cochrane, testified that she had been called to treat Dolan and found him suffering severe pain. *"Dr. Magee, she said, saw him every day and sometimes twice a day"*. She swore that Dolan needed a lot of liquor and stated *"that the patient was a headstrong man and demanded that he be allowed to pour his drinks himself. In the pouring of them, she testified, he spilt much of the liquor. At other times he became delirious and got up to pour a drink and spilled considerable [amounts] of his 'medicine'"*. In addition, it was not easy to obtain supplies quickly from the government dispensary in Ottawa and so she would order an additional prescription ahead of time whenever the stock began to get low. Nurse Cochrane's testimony did not persuade the magistrate who said that he was bound by the Ontario Temperance Act and had no choice but to find Charles guilty. A second similar charge against him was dropped.

Little more is known of this stay in Carp until, on 22 December 1921, Charles published this 'notice' in *The Carp Review*:

Dear Friends,

After serving you as promptly, efficiently and faithfully as lay in my power for seven years before the war and almost three years since, I have decided upon a special course. It has been difficult to find a satisfactory successor, but after steady and persistent effort I have secured Dr. W.G. Robertson of Renfrew. He graduated in 1916 and has five years training since, having spent two years in the Canadian Army Medical Corps in France, and since the war was senior house surgeon in Hamilton General Hospital for a year-and-a-half and afterwards took post graduate work in women's and children's diseases in Soho Hospital, Great Ormond Street and London General, London, England.

He comes highly recommended from the chiefs of these hospitals and I am pleased to leave my clientele to a man whom I believe to be reliable and conscientious. Dr. Robertson is here to stay and has decided to adjust his professional fees to the trend of the times.

He takes over my office and as I have always kept an accurate record of every case and its treatment, I leave the same for his reference so he begins where I left off. I hope to see many of you before I leave in order to have you meet Dr. Robertson and I trust you will see fit to accord him the same loyalty I have enjoyed.

Yours sincerely
C.F. Magee

According to Charles' sister, Bella, it was at this point that he was encouraged by a friend to look at work prospects in the U.S.A. In 1922, he travelled to Moscow, Idaho, where he eventually settled, practising medicine and teaching part-time at the University of Idaho.

On 3 April 1926, Charles married Dawn Hume, a nurse from Nelson (BC), born in 1894 in New Brunswick of a Methodist family. Their wedding took place in Nelson in the United Church. Charles registered himself as "divorced". Together, they opened and operated a private hospital ('Inland Empire Hospital') in Moscow. They lived at 325 N. Polk, an imposing house in the centre of Moscow.

Inland Empire Hospital (Moscow, Idaho)

Dr. Charles F. Magee and his wife, Dawn Hume, outside the Inland Empire Hospital

In 1933, Charles became a partner in the "Psychiana" Institute based in Moscow, Idaho, and run by Frank Robinson. His job was to provide 'mail order' medical diagnoses for any of the thousands of "Psychiana" devotees who requested (and paid for) them, and send the appropriate medication (cash on delivery). This episode is one of the stranger moments in a life filled with extraordinary events and experiences. **[see Appendix (p.83) for the story of "Psychiana".]**

In September 1935, Charles was appointed "Junior Grand Deacon" in the Masonic Grand Lodge of Idaho. He had already purchased a large, mixed farm near Genesee, about 25 km south of Moscow, where he raised purebred Hereford cattle. He later operated a dairy there and went into the purebred Guernsey cattle business. His nephew, Dr. William Gibson, spent the summer of 1933 helping run the farm. Charles gave him the two-volume *Life of Sir William Osler* by Harvey Cushing, which he read by kerosene lamp after the day's work was done.

Charles returned to Canada from time to time, visiting his sister, Bella, and her husband, during the summer. In 1944, they spent three weeks together at a cottage owned by the Gibson family on the Gatineau River.

Dr. Charles Franklin Magee died in Moscow at 9:30 p.m. on Monday, 11 February 1946, after suffering "acute myocarditis, with cardiac failure", resulting from influenza and a history of hypertensive cardio-vascular renal disease. His body was cremated in Spokane (Washington) on 15 February 1946. He was 70 years old.

Mary McGee

Mary McGee with Charlie on his 5th birthday (11 January 1916)

Mary quickly settled into her new life with Charlie. They lived in Brockton (Mass.), where Mary found work with the Brockton Visiting Nurse Association (founded in 1904). She was already using the form 'McGee' for her name and Charlie took on the name 'Charles Joseph McGee'. On 3 October 1916, Mary spoke at a public hearing on health insurance in Boston. Her friend, Mary Beard, was also there and took part in the discussions.

The Spanish Influenza arrived in Boston in late August 1918. On 3 September 1918, a young soldier from Brockton, home on leave, was among the first to be diagnosed. The disease spread rapidly and by October there had been a number of deaths and it was evident that Brockton was being particularly hard hit. A call for volunteers went out and a major effort was immediately under way to fight the epidemic, involving a large number of doctors and nurses. In every respect, the crisis was treated as a war effort, with frequent reference to the *"front line trenches"*. On 4 October 1918, it was decided to establish a field hospital in order to centralise resources and treatment. Within a few days, tents were in place with a capacity for 200 beds.

Brockton Field Hospital (8 October 1918).
Photo appears in Ernest Burrill's book, The Story of Brockton's Fight Against Influenza'
(1918, 39 pp.). The book covers the period September-October 1918.

The Nurses

Long before the volunteer organization was formed the burden of the epidemic fell heavily upon the staff of the visiting nurse association. The first case came to their attention on September 13, rapidly followed by many others until the staff was overwhelmed with calls. The work was efficiently directed by Mrs. Mary McGee who remained loyally on duty until she herself fell victim to the disease on September 20. Mrs. McGee returned to her duties on October 6th when the work was at its height and her services were of incalculable value in directing this most important branch of the relief work. For weeks after the volunteer organization was dissolved the Visiting Nurse Association continued their work of mercy among the convalescents.

Eight nurses died as a result of the influenza. They are remembered in these words: *"With heroism and valor not exceeded by those participating in the great battles overseas, these brave women sacrificed their all that others might live"*. Mary's work and tireless energy were noted and she helped bring in nurses from elsewhere, including five from Toronto and nine from Halifax. During the few weeks that the field hospital operated, more than 300 patients were received, including almost 40 children.

In the Brockton area, between 30 September and 15 October 1918, a total of 2,248 patients were treated. Of these 256 died. Worldwide, 50 million people died during the course of the pandemic. In the US alone, more than 675,000 died, more than five times the number of American soldiers killed in the Great War.

Mary went on to become the Superintendent (Director) of the Brockton Visiting Nurse Association by 1929, a position she would hold for many years, until she retired in 1955 at the age of 70.

In October 1930, Mary was the centre of a major controversy involving the directors of the Brockton Visiting Nurse Association. Matters came to a head with the resignation of the president, several officers, and many directors (*"all of them leading clubwomen"*), who accused a small group of directors of supporting Mary who, they said, had opposed some organisation policies. The women's club movement had grown up throughout the U.S.A. in the 19th century, and, by the 1930s, had become an influential progressive movement associated with education and social reform.

Mary, on 14 October 1930, issued a signed statement reaffirming her loyalty to the president and to the association itself. The nursing committee of the association had refused to dismiss Mary at a meeting the previous week by a vote of 5 to 4. That decision was final. *The Boston Globe* (15 October 1930) reported that *"there has been much contention for months over Mrs. McGee, who, her critics admit, is capable and efficient, but is said not to be in harmony with some policies of some of the officers"*. Mary would remain as director of the Brockton Visiting Nursing Association for 25 more years.

Rev. Corbett McRae (one of Mary's cousins) died at her home in Brockton on 31 March 1940 at the age of 61. He had been parish priest at St. Alexander Church in Lochiel (Ontario) for 32 years. He had gone to Brockton several months earlier, hoping to be cured of his illness. His funeral took place in Alexandria on 3 April 1940. Mary and Charlie (now "Dr. McGee") travelled there for the occasion. This was one of several return visits to Glengarry.

The year before she died, Mary sent a letter on 3 March 1963 to her nephew, Archie, and his wife, Walburga ("Wallie"), who had written to her a month or two after they and their eleven children had moved from Biggar (Sask.) to Glen Nevis: *"I was very happy to have your most interesting letter about your doings and your wonderful happy family."* Mary went on to describe how *"the McLellans stole the secret of the Glen Nevis McRaes for tanning leather in the water of the River de Lisle"*. According to Mary, the McRaes (sons of John McRae and his wife, Mary McGillis) had to abandon their tanning interests and moved to Minnesota where they rose to prominence, becoming bankers, lawyers, and doctors.

She mentions her son, Charlie, who, at the time of writing, was a Lieutenant Colonel at Fort Sam Houston in San Antonio (Texas) taking a training course *"to learn new war tactics and such things [that] are essential to our security"*. Although Charlie was a hard worker, he was finding this course *"more difficult than medical school or Greek and Latin and trigonometry"*. There was a possibility that he might return to the Kimbrough Army Hospital in Fort Bragg (N. Carolina).

Mary concludes: *"As I approach the 79 year mark, I do enjoy good health and the arthritis from two fractures is no longer painful. May God love and protect you and your dear wife and all your children. My love to you all. Affectionately, your Aunt Mary McGee."*

Mary McGee died on 6 July 1964. It is probable that she was still in Brockton, but we have no information about her funeral nor where she is buried.

Charlie McGee

Charlie grew up with his mother in Brockton. It is possible that, in November 1927, he captained the Salem High School football team, playing left tackle. He graduated with a B.A. from Boston College on 10 June 1931. He then began his studies at Harvard Medical School, graduating in 1937. We know from the photos he took that, in June 1938, Charlie was in Bridge End visiting the McRaes who were still living there in the Brick House. He returned, with Mary, in 1940 for the funeral of Father Corbett McRae.

Charlie moved shortly afterwards to Jackson, Michigan, where, on 28 September 1944, he was married to Margaret Cecelia Folk (33) in St.John's Catholic Church. A daughter, Margaret Mary McGee, was born in 1948. In 1951, Charlie and Margaret spent some time in Brockton with Mary. Their home address in 1957 was still in Jackson (Michigan).

Charlie and daughter, Margaret Mary, in 1949.

Charlie enlisted in the U.S Army on 6 March 1951. He served in the Korean War (1950-53) and remained in the armed forces until 31 July 1971, when he was 60, and, having been in the military for twenty years, retired on full pension.

He lived his last years in Amador (California). We know nothing of Charlie's life during this time. His wife, Margaret, died in Jackson (Michigan) in 1991. I believe his daughter may have married Andy Pagnuelo. Charles Joseph McGee died in Sacramento on 11 August 1992.

Appendix: "Psychiana"

Man Can Talk With God Says Noted Psychologist

A new and revolutionary religious teaching based entirely on the misunderstood sayings of the Galilean Carpenter, and designed to show how we may find, understand and use the same identical power which Jesus used in performing his so-called miracles, is attracting world-wide attention to its founder, Dr. Frank B. Robinson, noted psychologist, author and lecturer. "Psychiana," this New Psychological Religion, believes and teaches that it is today possible for every normal human being, understanding spiritual law as Christ understood it, to duplicate every work that the Carpenter of Galilee ever did, even to raising the dead—it believes and teaches that when He said, "the things that I do shall Ye do also," He meant what He said and meant it literally to apply to all mankind, through all the ages.

Dr. Robinson has prepared a 6,000 word treatise on "Psychiana," in which he tells about his long search for the Truth, how he finally came to the full realization of the Unseen Power of force so dynamic in itself that all other powers and forces fade into insignificance beside it—how he learned to commune directly with the Living God, using this mighty never-failing power to demonstrate health, happiness, and financial success, and how any normal being may find and use it as Jesus did. He is now offering this treatise free to every reader of this paper who writes him. If you want to read this highly interesting revolutionary and fascinating story of the discovery of a great Truth, just send your name and address to Dr. Frank B. Robinson, 16 Main St., Moscow, Idaho. It will be sent free and postpaid without cost or obligation. Write the Doctor today.—Advertisement.

In early 1930, this advertisement appeared in *Psychology* magazine. Astonishingly, over 5,000 people replied. Frank Robinson, born in 1886 in England, spent his early years in Yorkshire, where his father was a Baptist minister. His stepmother was abusive and, after a series of confrontations, Frank (17) and his younger brother, Sydney (15), were sent to Canada in 1903. They found work on a farm and eventually went separate ways. Frank was working in a pharmacy in Belleville (Ontario) in 1908, but moved on to Toronto and joined the Royal Northwest Mounted Police. He was dismissed two months later for excessive drinking, and then travelled to Vancouver and Victoria.

Frank Robinson entered the United States in 1910, continuing to find work as a pharmacist until he joined the army, under an assumed name. He still had serious drinking problems, was discharged, and moved to California and then to Oregon. He was somehow cured of his alcoholism and he married Pearl Leavitt in 1919. A son, Alfred, was born in 1923. After a series of moves around the States, the family settled in Moscow (Idaho) in April 1928, where Frank worked in the Corner Drugstore. A daughter, Florence, was born in January 1931.

It was at this time that Robinson developed his "new psychological religion" which he named "Psychiana". He recruited followers through advertisements placed in popular magazines, local newspapers, radio stations, and occasional public lectures, promising to send regular "lessons" and guidance for achieving health, wealth, and happiness, in return for modest subscriptions. It was one of the first "mail order" enterprises to succeed on a mass scale.

In spite of vigorous opposition from mainline churches, whose teachings Robinson dismissed as irrelevant and fundamentally wrong, "Psychiana" flourished and grew into a huge organisation. His teachings became increasingly popular and his emphasis on positive thinking, self-help, and material prosperity was well received by many people during these years of the Great Depression. Robinson continued working at the Moscow drugstore for about two years, while creating his newsletter teachings in his 'spare time', having them printed, and mailing them out on a regular basis. By any measure, his output was astonishing.

At its peak, the teachings were being mailed to over 600,000 "students" in 67 countries, with a million pieces of mail being sent out each year. "Psychiana" was reported as the seventh largest religion in the USA, employing nearly one hundred people (mostly women), and handling up to 50,000 pieces of mail per day. Robinson also developed a series of radio programs which were broadcast nationwide in the mid-1930s. He continued delivering public lectures and wrote 28 books.

By 1933, Robinson acquired his own printing operation and established Moscow's second daily newspaper, the *News Review*, which later merged with its rival, the *Star-Mirror*, to form *The Daily Idahonian*. The huge volume of mail resulted in the Moscow Post Office having to move to larger facilities. It is unclear where or how Robinson acquired the D.D. and the

Ph.D. that he used after his name, but it is speculated that he received them from a correspondence school operated by the College of Divine Metaphysics in Indianapolis.

It was at this time of greatest success that Frank Robinson persuaded Charles Magee to join him and together, in 1933, they set up the "Psychiana Clinic". It is not known how long Charles maintained his involvement in "Psychiana", but it seems likely that it lasted no more than a year or two. He presumably earned a sizeable income during this time.

"Psychiana" survived for almost twenty years although without the phenomenal success of the 1930s. Robinson ran into legal problems, including accusations of mail fraud, but he had powerful and influential friends who protected him and kept him clear of justice. After he died in 1948, his wife and family attempted to keep the business going, but without success and "Psychiana" was closed down by the early 1950s.

"PSYCHIANA" CLINIC

I am happy to inform my students that there now exists in Moscow a beautiful Clinic where the best medical and surgical advice of which we are capable may be obtained by our students. This Clinic has been in the back of my mind ever since I first released this teaching to the world. I knew it would come some day and built this movement with that in mind. Before many years this Clinic and its works will be known the entire world over, for here the scientific and ethical practice of medicine and surgery will be combined with the healing power of the Living God. That's an ideal combination.

A person would be very foolish to state that medicine and surgery are never necessary, and many a one has gone down to a premature grave through such fallacious belief. I grant you that the power of God is quite able to heal every conceivable sort of illness or disease where the law governing such healing is complied with. Given the proper faith there is no disease that can withstand the healing touch of the Spirit of God. Many people forget though that the Spirit of Truth or the Spirit of God has manifested through illumined physicians and surgeons the remedy for many diseases. Then again there are many who for some reason or other are unable to have sufficient faith in God to cast out the illnesses that seem to so easily beset them.

As you know, a few years ago I received a letter saturated with diphtheria germs and as a result of this letter all of my family came down with a very malignant type of this dreaded disease, and we all came nearly passing out of the picture. Now do you think for one moment that all I did was to pray for healing? If you do you are mistaken. I sent for the very man who now is in charge of our Clinic—Dr. Magee. Dr. Magee is one of the most conscientious and competent medical men I have ever seen. I knew that there was a specific for diphtheria, and you could not get me to that specific fast enough, for I knew that if given early enough in the disease, a cure is almost certain. Had I not have used medical advice and had I not taken the anti-diphtheritic serum I should not have been here and able to write this message to you.

At some time or other in the past, illumined physicians, experimenting with the deadly germ of diphtheria, found that the preparation of a serum from the anti-bodies was an almost sure specific. As a result of these experimentations and as a result of the discovery of the serum, thousands of lives have been saved from the dread ravages of this disease. I say to you that there is just as much of the Spirit of God in that diphtheria serum discovery and its results as there is in the cases which we have which respond without any treatment at all. I think perhaps that the vast majority of cases writing me for spiritual aid have had the very best medical advice possible. Almost always there is a competent physician in charge of the case.

Then, when medical help and advice seems to be failing, these good folks wire me and in practically every case the power of the Spirit of God is thrown against these diseases, and the patients recover. Now let us suppose that I received this morning a call that some student of mine was dying of some disease or other, and had no physician in attendance. The first thing I would insist on would be that the best medical advice obtainable be consulted. I should consider myself a criminal if I tried to do something through the realm of God directly when the remedy for the disease already was in existence. And everyone is foolish not to obtain the best medical advice possible in every case of real illness. Then it is, when medical help has failed, that the Spirit of God and its healing power can, and will, and does step into the picture and do in advance of medical knowledge what is needed to be done. Surely the remedy for every illness and disease lies somewhere in the realm of God. Of course it does. Medical science has gone a long way towards discovering the law governing the physical treatment of all illnesses. But medical science has not gone all the way.

There are more discoveries to be made yet. And I honor the men who are giving so freely of their time and money to the investigation of disease, for eventually they will discover what the Law of God is in all diseases and their cure. *But until the time comes when we know the answer to the problem of illness, and after the physician has done what he can, then we must obtain our help direct from the Spirit of God Itself.* And that is exactly what our Clinic is doing.

Where only medical treatment or surgical treatment is necessary, it will be rendered by Dr. Magee and his capable assistants in as careful and scientific a manner as possible. Then, when medical science can do no more, the spiritual help of the Power of God will be called into play, and in the name of this mighty Life Spirit, we shall endeavor to conquer these pesky diseases. For great is the power of the Life Spirit when only a little confidence is shown in it.

In choosing Dr. Magee for Chief Surgeon of the Clinic I am particularly fortunate in being able to obtain him for he has conducted this same hospital privately for many years and has been eminently successful. Dr. Magee is known throughout the entire Inland Empire as perhaps the cleverest physician and surgeon we have. He is a man of deep religious convictions and more than that, he has an abiding faith in God, and when you find a physician who recognizes the fact that the Spirit of God is behind all healings, you are fortunate. Dr. Magee is a graduate of McGill University in Montreal, Canada, and after that a graduate of the University of Vienna. He also is a member of both the Canadian and American Medical Associations. Best of all, though, he recognizes his union with the Spirit of Life, and, putting forth the very best efforts he can, and coupling them with his superior medical and surgical training, there is no wonder that he has been so successful.

This Clinic will soon be know all over the world, and Moscow will not be able to accommodate the people who come here for treatment both physical and spiritual. There is at the present time a move on foot for the building of a three or four hundred-bed hospital, and this will be enlarged still further as the need arises. At the present time we can accommodate about thirty patients here. Remember please in this new movement that the Spirit of God, which Spirit has led us thus far, will be given complete charge of the Clinic. Not a move will be made which is not in harmony with the Spirit of God as we understand it. Whatever results are achieved here will be due

directly to the healing power of God coupled with the ethical and scientific practice of medicine and surgery. Where medicine cannot help, the Spirit of God can help, and will help just as long as we retain our confidence and faith in the great Life Spirit we have learned to know and love so well.

We are making the charges at the Clinic as reasonable as we possibly can. I have no surplus money and therefore this Clinic must be on a self-supporting basis. I am not interested in making money out of it. All it will be asked to do is to pay its way, and therefore we are adopting a system of charging which is eminently fair. In all operative cases and in all cases where physio-therapy or X-ray or other treatments are indicated, they will be charged for at the regular rates set by the American Medical Association. The rate for a private room at the Clinic will be only $5.00 a day including meals. A ward bed may be secured for $3.00 a day. Whatever medicines may be necessary will be provided and charged for extra. Right on the start we shall not be able to care for those who unfortunately are not in a position to meet our charges. Perhaps later we shall have a department for taking care of such cases. But not having surplus funds, and having lost all our three accounts recently in a bank failure, this department cannot be considerd until such time as we are financially able to do so.

Now, for the benefit of those students who cannot come to Moscow to this Clinic, we have brought into existence a Mail Consultation Department for the benefit of our students. This department, as the Clinic proper, is only for our students. The facilities of the Clinic, and the Mail Consultation Department are not available to the public. At least not yet. When advice by mail is requested, a diagnosis blank is provided, and my students may have the benefit of Dr. Magee's advice or that of his assistants at nominal cost. The charge for the initial diagnosis is only $5.00 whereas many large hospitals charge as high as $65.00. We do not want to make any money out of our students though, so we are holding this diagnosis charge down to the very minimum. Additional advice will be charged for at the rate of $2.50 per consultation. Where medicines are necessary they will be sent from here to the patient C. O. D. I own a drug store in Moscow and will see that the charges for these medicines are as low as is consistent with good business.

Already many have applied for accommodations at the Clinic, and many more have taken advantage of our Mail Consultation Department. It is quite necessary that applications for accommodations at the Clinic be made in advance. Please do not come here for treatment until such arrangements have been made. Moscow has two hotels, and there are private homes where rooms for relatives may be had at a reasonable charge. We plan to build our own hotel in the future, but at the present time there are ample accommodations here for those who come to us.

I want to ask every student of mine to affirm for the outstanding success of this new movement. It will be successful whether or no. But there are tens of thousands of students in tune with the Infinite God, and where their desires are all for a certain thing, and where that thing is for the good of the human race, there cannot be failure. Personally I don't know what the word failure means since I literally stepped out on the sure and safe promises of God. For there is no failure where God is known and trusted I assure you. However—here is the Clinic. It has been arranged for in the light of, and under the guidance of the Great Life Spirit, and, as with "PSYCHIANA" its light and help will go around the world in short order. Thousands will be helped. And this will make me glad and happy.

You will remember that 2,000 years ago one evening, when the sun was setting, they brought to the greatest Spiritual Teacher this world has ever known, all those who were afflicted with pains and divers diseases. And He healed them. From out that great heart there went forth sufficient of the power of God to demonstrate the power of God over all material things, including illnesses and sicknesses. No manner of disease was able to withstand that divine touch. And no manner of disease is able to withstand that touch today. It is true that there were places in which the great Master of Spiritual healing could do none of His wonderful works, *because of their unbelief*. And there will still be those on whom we cannot demonstrate the Power of the Spirit of God— because of their unbelief. But I can promise you that if there is faith as big as a grain of

mustard seed in the Living God—*the results will be sure.*

A great number of my students complain of some physical ailment or other, and to these I advise a consultation with Dr. Magee or his assistants. Address all mail matter for the Clinic or for Dr. Magee to "PSYCHIANA" CLINIC, Box 399, Moscow, Idaho, and be sure and make reservations in advance if you intend to come here. Also hold up this new venture before the great God of the universe, and as we succeed in this healing movement you will have the satisfaction of knowing that you have done your little bit towards helping us.

ABOLISH SUNDAY SCHOOLS, RELIGIOUS BODY IS TOLD.

Cincinnati, May 4.—(AP)—Suggestions that would drastically alter or possibly replace a long-standing institution—the Sunday school—were placed before the Religious Education Association delegates today.

Dr. Adelaide Case of Columbia University teachers' college said she felt Sunday schools were retarding religious progress, and proposed creation of community groups of wider scope.

Rabbi Isaac Landman of New York, editor of the American Hebrew, called sunday schools, as now constituted, breeders of agnosticism and atheism, and the "greatest weakness" and "most costly liability" of the church.

Dr. Case said she doubted whether the average Sunday school program was effective enough to warrant continuation. Rabbi Landman suggested wholesale revision of Sunday schools and reinterpretation of the Ten Commandments.

He said their literal inhibition against idolatory and affirmation of the "six-day creation myth were of no value in building character and inculcating intellectual honesty."

The association took no immediate steps to incorporate these suggestions into the policies being fomulated.

Rabbi Landman said:

"Even where adults attend the Sunday school, they are fed on mythical tales, goody-goody maxims and intellectual one-half of one per cent pap."

"PSYCHIANA" CLINIC

A private institution devoted to the ethical and scientific practice of Medicine and Surgery as an adjunct to the healing power of the Spirit of God.

LOCATED AT MOSCOW, IDAHO

(86 miles from Spokane, Wash., on the Great Northern, Northern Pacific, and Union Pacific Railways)

FRANK B. ROBINSON, PH.D., M.Sc., D.D.
SPIRITUAL ADVISOR

CHAS. F. MAGEE, M.D., C.M.
CHIEF SURGEON

THE CLINIC

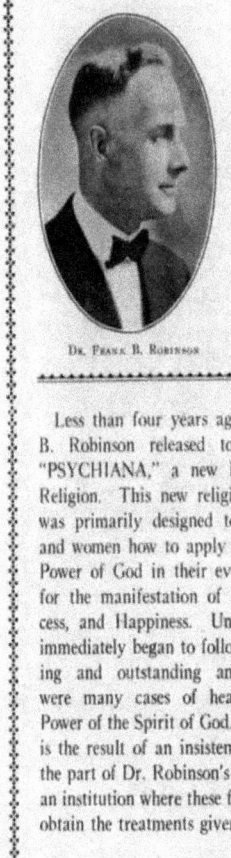

IS EQUIPPED WITH EVERY REQUISITE OF MEDICINE AND SURGERY. X-RAY, PHYSIOTHERAPY AND OPERATIVE T R E A T M E N T ROOMS. CLINICAL LABORATORY AND COMPLETE DIAGNOSIS FACILITIES.

Dr. Frank B. Robinson

Dr. C. F. Magee

Less than four years ago Dr. Frank B. Robinson released to the world "PSYCHIANA," a new Psychological Religion. This new religious teaching was primarily designed to teach men and women how to apply the Spiritual Power of God in their everyday lives, for the manifestation of Health, Success, and Happiness. Unusual results immediately began to follow this teaching and outstanding amongst them were many cases of healing by the Power of the Spirit of God. This Clinic is the result of an insistent demand on the part of Dr. Robinson's followers for an institution where these followers may obtain the treatments given here.

DR. CHAS. F. MAGEE

is considered by Dr. Robinson to be one of the most capable physicians and surgeons on the Pacific Coast. A graduate of McGill University, Montreal, Canada, and later of the University of Vienna. A member of the Canadian and American Medical Associations Dr. Magree's ability is well known and recognized, and his outstanding Chrisian life demonstrates his unassailable character. In his very successful practice of medicine and surgery, he recognizes that all healing comes from the Spirit of God and in this realization he applies his knowledge of medicine and surgery withoutstanding success.

SPECIAL NOTE

The facilities of this Clinic including the Mail Consultation Department are for the use of Students of "PSYCHIANA" only. They are not available to the public. It is necessary that a reasonable charge be made for the services of the Clinic as it must be kept self-supporting. Should there be those who are not satisfied with the advice by mail given thru the Mail Consultation Department, if they will immediately notify us to that effect we will be happy to refund the amount paid for that advice. We are not interested in making money. All we are trying to do is to help our Students in as intelligent a manner as possible.

THE CLINIC ... ITS PURPOSE

"PSYCHIANA" Clinic is an institution for the scientific medical and surgical treatment of the human body and mind under the supervision of the most competent physicians and surgeons we can find. It is conducted according to the highest standards of medical ethics and scrupulous care is given to see that these standards are observed.

This Clinic is an affiliation of "PSYCHIANA" and was brought into being to accommodate those demanding advice of Dr. Frank B. Robinson, the founder of "PSYCHIANA." With the release of this new religious teaching, there was demonstrated beyond a doubt that spiritual or so-called "divine" healing is an actual fact. This is nothing new. Spiritual healing has been an accomplished fact for many years, and every reputable physician recognizes the fact that there is a greater law behind this universe than the law of medicine.

This Clinic recognizes the fact that in the last analysis all healing comes from the creative intelligence behind this universe. It recognizes the fact that when medical science has done what it can do, often spiritual or divine power steps in and accomplishes what medicine or surgery have failed to accomplish. We believe, however, that the scientific and conscientious practice of medicine and surgery is just as much a part of divine or spiritual law as is the healing which occurs without medical treatment, or after medical science has done all it can do.

It is manifestly wrong to expect spiritual or divine power to effect any healing, if the means of healing for that particular ailment have already been provided. In many cases looking for spiritual or divine healing, all that is necessary is intelligent, competent, medical or surgical treatment. It is the purpose of this Clinic to provide just that. Where spiritual aid alone is desired, this will be provided without charge by Dr. Robinson, provided everything that medical science can do has been done. Where medical or surgical relief is indicated, this will be rendered by competent medical men under the direct supervision of Dr. Magee.

CLINIC RATES

SINGLE ROOMS (Meals included) .... $5.00 per day
WARD BEDS (Meals included) .... 3.00 per day
PRIVATE NURSE .... 5.00 per day
(All fees payable in advance)

Physio-Therapy, X-Ray, Operative Treatments, Diagnosis, etc., are charged for at regular American Medical Association rates.
All medicines are extra.

For the benefit of those unable to attend the Clinic, a Mail Consultation Department exists. Diagnosis blanks for mail consultations furnished by the Clinic at no cost.

Reservations at the Clinic must be made in advance. Shortly a very much larger Clinic will be constructed having accommodations for several hundred beds.

'MAN CAN NOW TALK WITH GOD'
TEACHES NEW AMERICAN RELIGION

Health Restored — Earnings increased — Contentment Found. Dynamic Power Astounds "Psychiana" Followers. "In These Strenous Times I Know of Nothing That Will Give a Person More Hope than 'Psychiana'." Writes California Student.

"For 2,000 years," declares Dr. Frank B. Robinson, founder of "Psychiana," the new psychological religion, people have missed something in life and have sought it in many ways. Like many other great discoveries, my own grasp of this dynamic, universal Power came after many years of intense search. When the Truth broke upon me, I was staggered by its immensity. Yet it is so simple and clear that it can be easily understood and applied by any normal person."

Here is an absolutely new understanding of life and God—as modern in its application as radio or air travel.

Read what some "Psychiana" students have written—

"I cannot thank you too much for the Joy that this teaching brings to us. Our life has been completely changed in every way."

"'Psychiana' will be my religion always for I think it is wonderful. A great deal of good has come to us in the last two years and our needs seem to be met in the most unexpected and unusual ways."

"I am indebted to you for the spiritual realities brought to me through Psychiana. This spiritual awakening is absolutely matchless—like a spring whose waters cannot fail."

"I do not know how I could have existed the past year without Psychiana. It is solving one of the hardest problems of life for me and in a manner I couldn't have dreamed of two years ago."

Underwood & Underwood

DR. FRANK B. ROBINSON
Founder of "Psychiana"

"I wonder what would this world be like, if the Truth as it is revealed in Psychiana could be in every home."

"Psychiana" is obvious that every American family know what this new religion is accomplishing in the lives of thousands. You may think you are not interested in religion—you may have tried them all and still be unsatisfied—but wouldn't you like to know just what this great new Teaching actually does?

We will be glad to send you Dr. Robinson's booklet in which he tells of his long search for the Truth and how he learned to commune directly with the Living God and to use this mighty, never-failing power to demonstrate health, happiness and financial success. There will be no obligation. Send your name and address to "The Church of Psychiana," 22-1616 Street, Moscow, Idaho. Write for it today. Copyright, 1926, "Psychiana," Inc., a religious institution chartered by the State of Idaho.—[Advertisement]

"Psychiana" button: Frank Robinson's contribution to the war effort.

Bibliography

Newspapers: The Glengarry News, The Carp Review, Cornwall Standard, Ottawa Citizen, Ottawa Journal, The Toronto World, Toronto Daily Star, The Province [Vancouver], The Vancouver Daily World, Vancouver Sun, Edmonton Journal, Manitoba Free Press, Lethbridge Herald, The Morning Leader [Regina], Evening Record [Windsor], The Boston Globe.

https://www.ancestry.com/

https://www.newspapers.com/

http://www.cmp-cpm.forces.gc.ca/dhh-dhp/his/le-lr/mu-um-eng.asp
Record of Service (C.A.M.C. Medical Units)

http://www.iapsop.com/archive/materials/psychiana/

Glengarry County Archives (Alexandria, Ontario)

The Glengarry Archives (Sir John Johnson Manor House, Williamstown, Ontario)

Huntley Township Historical Society

Library of Parliament (Canada)

Library and Archives (Canada)

Ernest Burrill, *The Story of Brockton's Fight Against Influenza* (1918, 39 pp.)

G. W. L. Nicholson, *Canadian Expeditionary Force 1914-1919* (1962, 676 pp.)

Allan D. Scott, *History of 11 (Victoria) Field Ambulance and its predecessors* (2009)

"Psychiana" Quarterly (June 1933, 36 pp.

Chronography

- 13 August 1875: Charles Magee born in North Gower (Ontario)
- 9 September 1884: Mary McRae born in Bridge End (Ontario)
- 1899: Charles enters McGill medical school
- 1902: Mary enters nursing school in Ottawa
- 1903: Charles graduates from McGill
- 1904: Charles opens medical practice in Carp (Ontario)
- 8 June 1905: Mary graduates from school of nursing
- 8 March 1906: Charles purchases Carp drugstore
- 1906: Mary begins work as nursing assistant with Charles in Carp
- 19 April 1908: *Ne Temere* papal decree takes effect
- 21 October 1908: Charles and Mary are married in Chicago
- 20 January 1910: Mary leaves Charles for the first time
- 1910: Charles hires William Shaw as drugstore manager
- 7 May 1910: Mary leaves Charles for the second time
- 11 January 1911: Charlie born in Carp
- 3 May 1911: Mary leaves Charles for the third and final time
- 7 May 1911: Charlie baptised in Glen Nevis
- 1 July 1911: Charles attempts to seize Charlie in Bridge End, and William Shaw is shot
- 7 July 1911: William Shaw dies in Cornwall Hospital
- 15 July 1911: Farquhar McRae committed for trial
- 24 October 1911: Farquhar's trial begins in Cornwall
- 28 October 1911: Farquhar sentenced to life imprisonment
- 1 November 1911: Farquhar taken to Kingston Penitentiary
- 6 December 1911: Charles unsuccessfuly seeks legal custody of Charlie
- 23 December 1911: D.C. McRae (72) dies in Bridge End
- 15 April 1912: sinking of the *Titanic*
- 18 April 1912: Charles kidnaps Charlie in Ottawa
- June 1912: Charles is in Vienna and meets Phila Marton
- 29 June 1912: Farquhar released following petition to Minister of Justice
- 22 August 1912: Charles and Phila are 'betrothed' in Vienna
- 30 September 1912: Charles and Phila arrive in Toronto
- 6 October 1912: Charles, Phila, and Charlie cross B.C. border into Idaho
- 1913: Charles, Phila, and Charlie settle in Vancouver

- 29 September 1914: Phila brings formal charges against Charles in Vancouver
- 2 November 1914: Mary 'kidnaps' Charlie and returns to Ontario
- 19 November 1914: Charles is on trial, but jury fails to reach a decision
- 27 November 1914: Charles is tried for a second time but, again, no decision
- December 1914: Mary and Charlie move to Brockton, near Boston
- 24 March 1915: Charles loses lawsuit against Phila to regain his property
- 3 May 1915: All charges against Charles are dropped
- 12 August 1915: Charles enlists to serve in France
- December 1915: Charles travels to England
- 1916: Mary begins her career with the Brockton Home Nursing Association
- 1916-1918: Charles in France and England
- September 1918: Spanish influenza reaches Brockton
- September-October 1918: Mary helps the fight against influenza in Brockton
- 18 October 1918: Charles is back in Vancouver from Europe
- 1919: Charles re-opens his medical practice in Carp
- 22 December 1921: Charles announces that he is leaving Carp
- 1922: Charles travels to Moscow (Idaho), where he settles
- 3 April 1926: Charles marries Dawn Hume
- 1933: Charles works for "Psychiana"
- 1937: Charlie graduates from Harvard Medical School
- 28 September 1944: Charlie marries Margaret Folk in Jackson (Michigan)
- 1948: Margaret Mary McGee is born
- 11 February 1946: Charles dies in Moscow (Idaho)
- 1951: Charlie enlists in U.S. army and serves in Korea
- 1955: Mary retires from her position as Director of the Home Nursing Association
- 6 July 1964: Mary dies in Brockton
- 1971: Charlie retires from military service
- 11 August 1992: Charlie (Charles Joseph McGee) dies in Sacramento

Family Trees

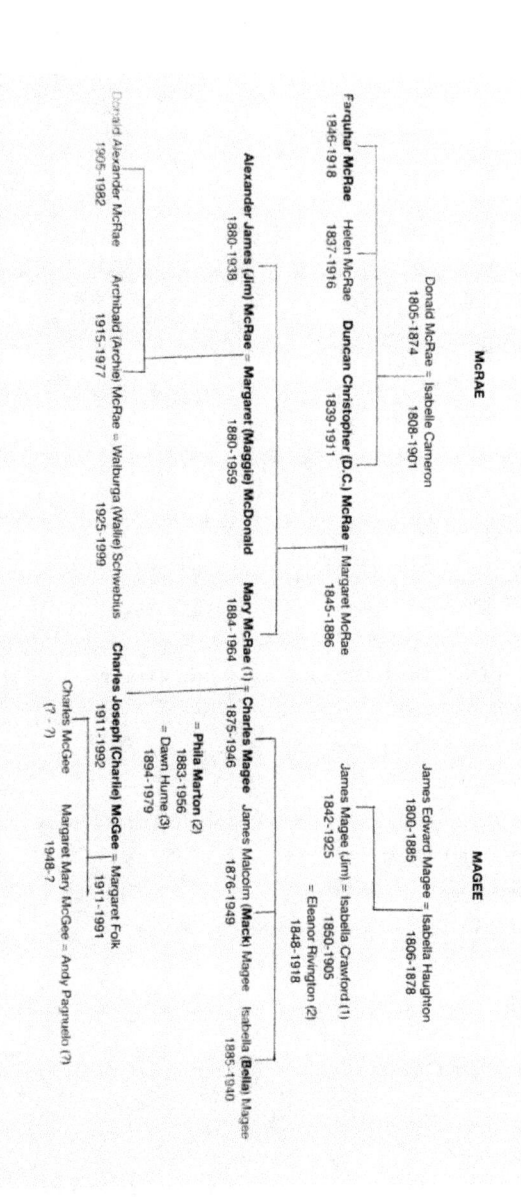

About the author

Roger Clark was born in Middlesbrough (Yorkshire) in 1939, a few months before the outbreak of the Second World War. In 1950 he moved with his family to Exeter (Devon), where he was a pupil at Hele's Grammar School. He went to university in London (King's College), where he completed a B.A. Honours degree in French and German, including one year teaching English at the Lycée Jacques Amyot in Auxerre.

After graduating, he travelled to Canada in 1962, where he completed an M.A. in 18th-century French literature at McMaster University in Hamilton (Ontario). He took up a teaching post the following year at the University of Saskatchewan in Saskatoon. He was awarded a research grant in 1967 and spent two years in Paris carrying out post-graduate work on 18th-century French utopian literature.

Returning to Canada in 1969, he taught French language and literature at Memorial University of Newfoundland for the next eighteen years. For fifteen of those years he served as chair of the Department of French and Spanish. Together with a colleague from the University of Saskatchewan, he founded and directed a summer school in Trois-Rivières (Québec) from 1972-77. During this time, he published a number of scholarly articles on French utopian literature.

In 1987, he left the academic world and moved to Ottawa to join the professional staff of Amnesty International (Canada). He was appointed Secretary General in 1988 and remained in that position until his retirement in December 1999. He participated in numerous research missions for the organisation, including the investigation of human rights violations in Cambodia (1991 and 1993), Rwanda and Zaire (1995 and 1996), as well as Burundi, Guatemala, Liberia, Ethiopia, Nepal, and Algeria. In 1997-98, he served as Interim Director of Amnesty International's Africa Program based at the International Secretariat in London. He was appointed a Member of the Order of Canada in 2001 for his human right work and the following year was awarded an honorary doctorate at St. Thomas University (New Brunswick).

He is a passionate bird watcher and continues working to promote human rights and climate justice. He is the author of two books: *Beautiful with Birds* (2015) and *Scribbler* (2018). He is married to Pat McRae and lives in Ottawa. They have five children and ten grandchildren.

Contact: erogclark@gmail.com

CPSIA information can be obtained
at www.ICGtesting.com
Printed in the USA
LVHW032106060120
642662LV00014B/2190/P